Beyond the Bubble

Beyond the Bubble

9 Market-Proof Power Plays for Women who Want to Invest in Real Estate

Latisha B. Gray

iUniverse, Inc.
New York Lincoln Shanghai

Beyond the Bubble
9 Market-Proof Power Plays for Women who Want to Invest in Real Estate

iUniverse books may be ordered through booksellers or by contacting:

iUniverse
2021 Pine Lake Road, Suite 100
Lincoln, NE 68512
www.iuniverse.com
1-800-Authors (1-800-288-4677)

ISBN-13: 978-0-595-40436-0 (pbk)
ISBN-13: 978-0-595-84811-9 (ebk)
ISBN-10: 0-595-40436-7 (pbk)
ISBN-10: 0-595-84811-7 (ebk)

Printed in the United States of America

Acknowledgements

Through tears, frustration, doubt, and low valleys, God has brought me through to fruit—a finished product. I lift this work up to you, Lord, and I hope and pray that it will be used to help someone find the confidence to follow their dreams and deliver them into financial freedom.

To my husband, Scott, thank you for believing in me and never letting me stop moving forward to my goals. Thank you for being a great teacher and inspiration who taught me so much more about real estate than I would have ever ventured to discover on my own. It is because of you that I had the courage to move forward with buying my first investment property. You are a terrific business partner, friend, and husband. I dedicate this book, my life and success to you.

I'm also dedicating this book to my friend Tia and all my other girlfriends, business partners, sorors, and sisters everywhere who are striving to be financially independent. Continue with the struggle. It is up to all of us to pass down a legacy of strength, empowerment, and wealth to young sisters who will follow in our footsteps.

Finally, to my family, friends, former teachers, mentors, and coaches, thank you for the kind words, the encouraging notes, the smiles, the sense of belief. My life has been filled with a myriad of well wishers ready to give a lift when it was needed.

Contents

INTRODUCTION

Congratulations on starting onto the road to financial independence. I remember when my mind finally made a shift from financial dependence to the desire for independence. I was working with a real estate client who was also a friend who was pretty much in financial distress. He had terrible credit (a score in the low 500's), he was in debt, he was overwhelmed, he was stressed out, and he felt he was at the end of his rope.

One great thing about his financial situation was that he owned a little 3 Bedroom Single Family house in a pretty decent neighborhood. He had just evicted his mother who was living there and never paying the rent (this was part of his financial problem!). He consulted with me to see if I could help him. With my real estate expertise and amateur credit repairing skills, I was certain I could add some value. We pulled his credit and took a look. He had never pulled his credit report before. Although his score was low, we found that there were only a few accounts that were severely affecting his score. We worked a little on his credit report and were able to clear through much of his "credit clutter."

Also, we looked at his house. His mom was at least a pretty good housekeeper so the house was in pretty good shape. I convinced him to put on a fresh white coat of paint and spend $500 on freshening up the bathroom, tiling the kitchen floors, and cleaning the carpet. The house was ready to go. We listed it for about $20,000 more than he thought he could get for hit. Somehow he missed the market boom and didn't realize the increased value of his home.

After only a week, we had an offer that closed 30 days later. Sitting at the closing, my client/friend was presented with a check for $40,000. He was happy and told me this transaction changed the whole course and direction of his life. That comment meant so much to me. Before then, I can't recall anyone ever telling me that something I did "changed the whole course and direction of their life." It was amazing and completely inspiring. I thought to myself, can I do more. And if I can change his life, can I change mine?

That's when I truly realized the power of ownership, the power of equity, and the power of real estate. It occurred to me that if you duplicated this type of transaction over and over again, it wouldn't take very long to truly attain financial independence. I was hooked for a lifetime.

Since working with my friend Kelvin, I have had numerous clients to cash out their real estate investments and walk away with big checks. I've seen people leverage their real estate to achieve their biggest goals. I've seen my own life change. I realize that I can dream bigger than my job. I've realized that if I desire more in my life that I have the power to give it to myself through the power of God and the spirit of prosperity that is inside of me. And because of this realization, the question now becomes, what are you going to do?

If not now, When?

Now is the time to do something different, to have something more, and to be who we want to be. Have you ever hoped and dreamed so hard until you were just sick that things would change in your life. Maybe you're bank account has the same pitiful balance each time you check it or you keep wishing you could do something with your life if you only had money.

Money, that dreaded M word that haunts us when we don't have it. Money gives us visions of freedom, self expression, and happiness beyond our belief. This energy called money can zap us down when we don't have it, tie us to an unhappy job when we need it, and confuse us when we want it.

What were you doing ten years ago? Can you remember? Well according to a report in the USA Today, people who bought a house ten years ago saw their investment double. I imagine most of you have had many life experiences whether you have spent the last ten years as a renter or if you've own a home already. And because of your interest in this subject matter, you probably have an independent streak, have people who look up to you, and have people who count on you. How different would your life be now if you'd invested then and doubled your money? What could you do? What could you give?

This book will look at real estate investing as a way for you to infuse more money, more confidence, and more power in your life. This book is about real estate investing for women who are ready and willing to do something different. If you've thought about it but found reasons why it isn't for you, I challenge you to just open your mind because the potential for success is real, attainable, and achievable for any of us. Being ready and willing is a state of mind not a state of your pocket book.

Thank you for joining us on this journey to wealth. The time is surely now to get into the real estate game. We don't know what will happen in the next ten years but we do know that we and everyone we encounter has to have somewhere to live now and somewhere to live then. The question is how many of those properties will you own? When building equity, time is definitely on your side.

Part One

GET IN THE GAME

CHAPTER 1

Why Real Estate

Freedom is the number one reason to explore real estate investing as a woman seeking financial independence. Freedom from debt, freedom from a lifeless career, and freedom to define your own destiny are some of the direct benefits of a life as a successful real estate investor. Because most real estate is a "no brainer" investment, it's not even hard to be a success. As an investment, understanding real estate is simple and secure. The availability to have unlimited income is why I will always consider myself a real estate investor.

The advantages of entering the real estate game range from increasing financial security to improving your investment ability using a safe and proven investment. It's a game that anyone can enter and anyone can learn. It's simple, understandable and profitable. Real estate investing was like an old secret to success that all the rich people knew about but someone forgot to tell me. And from the variety of women I've encountered through my life, I realize that many of them didn't get the message either.

Perhaps, many of us heard it or knew it deep down but somehow felt that this form of investing did not apply to us or was not available to us. My goal is to show you otherwise. Stick with me and I can pretty much guarantee your success. But as the old saying goes, you can lead a horse to water but you can't make her drink. By the time you finish this book you should be at the water and have the confidence and assurance to drink. That's why the first part of this book is entitled "Get in The Game." Stop making excuses, Stop wondering if it is for you, start making yourself and your well being a priority and I promise your life will change.

If you've read this far, then you must be interested in improving your financial situation. And I'm a witness that change is possible through real estate investing and the tips and tricks that will be outlined in this book.

Who Should get into Real Estate?

Anytime a person desires more for there life, they have made themselves qualified to achieve a greater level of success. I'm a firm believer if you can conceive it and believe it then you can achieve it. In real estate, anyone can be successful if you just take a small chance to get into gear. Action anywhere is much better that inaction everywhere. Today, the challenge is to believe you can do it.

Once you have the vision and desire to become a real estate investor, the resources are out there to get started. Theses power plays are a compilation of many of the best practices of the top investors currently in the business. The tips I'm sharing are simple, easy to follow, and achievable to anyone who applies the techniques. Many techniques will never be shared with you by your lender or realtor because their motivations are different.

Many of the richest people today who weren't passed down wealth have gotten rich through the help of their real estate investments. Real estate investing is not a new process. In fact our forefathers staked their claim in the earth upon their arrival to the new world. They didn't ask the Americans for a rental lease but they took over and became owners. And because of their actions, their descendents have enjoyed the riches of what land ownership provides.

Real estate has consistently been the one of the best assets that will continue to appreciate over time. Why is real estate the best? Because they aren't making any more of it. Many of the richest families passed down assets to their heirs in the form of real estate. Even in a Housing Bubble, unless you're in a 10 million dollar cottage in LA, most real estate will continue to appreciate over time. And certainly, anywhere in the United States, there will always be a need for 3 Bedroom brick ranch in a nice affordable neighborhood.

We just finished with the Greenspan era where profits from real estate were obtained at record levels. Many fair weather investors are now wondering if making profits from real estate is a thing of the past. As get rich quick "fly by night" investors move out of the way, there is plenty of room for women to take the investment helm and win in this real estate game.

A Woman's Touch

Understanding the needs of families is just one reason why women and real estate are a natural fit. The style and detail nature associated with a "woman's touch" is a quality that can translate into big money for women interested in the real profession. Women have traditionally out performed and out numbered their male counterparts in residential home sales. But when it comes to commercial listings and investment properties, women have been less visible. My goal is to put an end to that trend.

Because traditionally women have chosen not to venture beyond residential sales, we have not adequately empowered ourselves or others. When in actuality, the same qualities that would make a woman a great realtor would also help to make her a great investor. Great realtors usually have a knack for pointing ways to help a home sell fast, great realtors create a win/win for the buyer and seller, and great realtors are committed to closing the deal—These are all the same great qualities needed by a successful investor. The only difference is that the investor becomes the buyer or the intercessory to the buyer but the goals are the same.

For women everywhere who are looking for a new challenge, new freedoms, and new income, I strongly suggest real estate investing because of its practicality and flexibility to fit into your lifestyle. And if you want great odds in achieving financial freedom and flexibility, real estate investing may be your best choice.

Why did I become interested in real estate and adding an additional stream of income into my household? In 1999 the huge auto manufacturer that I worked for started laying off, and although I was spared my job, many of my friends were not. I was appalled and offended by this type of vulnerability. I thought to myself that I had gone to college, moved away from my friends and family on two company transfers. I was spending a lot of time traveling for the company and sleeping in hotels and for what? For them to decide that if they wanted to they could lay me off at the drop of a hat.

I was very disheartened. I wasn't much different than my friends and it's very feasible that on another day a lay off could have been a part of my story. In a moment, I just made a decision that my story would never one of victimization or vulnerability if I could help it. I started looking around for a Plan B, for another alternative, and a vehicle to building wealth. I found the answer in real estate. It was something that was always there but I wasn't open to seeing the opportunities. At that moment, I was.

Achieve Your Financial Dreams

Real Estate can help you to achieve your financial dreams no matter how small or large. I meet women all the time who don't have the money to take fun, nurturing trips or those who always complain that money is tight and they don't know how they will make ends meet. Many of these women are professional and have 'good' jobs that they went to college to get several degrees for. Then seemingly at that the same time I've run across people who have no financial worries, they love what they are doing, and they seem to have sense of freedom to express themselves, to love, and to live. What's the difference? The difference lies in their ability to use money as a tool to help alleviate their financial stresses.

Financial disarray can lead to stress and worry unlike anything else. Eventually, I left my corporate job to sell real estate full time. When I sold real estate full time I often worked 14 to 16 hour days and because of my efforts, I made a decent living. However, I knew there had to be more. I was working too hard for a lot of bad deals. And at a time when I dipped into a financial valley, I stressed, gained weight and my business suffered. The lack of financial security was weakening me and I became very unhappy in a business that I once loved. I resolved this situation by taking another job and approaching real estate a lot differently.

Fortunately, for me, my real estate experiences inspired me to learn from my mistakes and approach the industry again from a position of power. How did I achieve this power? By making real estate work for me! I was able to sell my house and use the equity to buy an income generating property as well as pay off my debt. Wow, this was liberating.

If you've ever carried debt for multiple years, in my case around 10 years, you know the weight of this burden. Releasing this weight was my first step to financial independence. The steps in this book are designed to show others how to release that same weight that may be in their lives. There are several methods, plans and ideas can lead you on a path to financial independence. Some of these factors are saving, reducing you're spending, living within a budget, reducing your debt, increasing your income, and more. This book is not intended to discount any positive action that you are currently implementing. This book intends to show you how and why you should invest in real estate. A great solution to many of my income concerns and debt concerns were resolved by the equity I earned investing in real estate. Real estate can help you alleviate debt, can help finance your career goals, can provide financial freedom in times of need. That's why I strongly believe that real estate can be your ticket to financial happiness.

Achieve Your Entrepreneurial Dreams

Investing in real estate can provide financial freedom from debt but can also be a source to fund any entrepreneurial dreams that you may have. Many business owners are able to successfully launch a business by using the equity in their homes. The founder of BET and Charlotte Bobcat owner, Bob Johnson, reportedly used a $50,000 Home Equity line of credit to start BET which he later sold to Viacom Media for 1 Billion Dollars. What a story. Unfortunately, unless someone taught us this concept or we grew up seeing these types of deals being made, many of us just don't get it until way too late in life.

Now, I certainly can't promise that investing your home equity into your business will make you a billionaire but I do know you can increase your income by pretty much any amount you choose. You can make thousands of dollars off of houses you invest in and sell. You can earn returns on your money faster than any money market, life insurance, or mutual fund. You can easily enter this business on borrowed money and walk away with a profit. There are a ton of benefits that real estate can provide and set you on a course to financial security and independence.

I remember clearly sitting on my couch of my newly purchased home when I was 24 meeting with a financial planner/insurance salesman about my future. When I told him, I intended to be an entrepreneur one day he looked at my bleak financial situation and remarked "How are you going to do that?" His solution, save in a money market account and purchase cash value whole life insurance that I could borrow against years down the road after I paid so much in. With his advice, I started saving and started to think about investing, however, this information was not going to help me with my "right-now" need to make some money.

In fact, I looked at this policy the other day and realized that after 7 years of diligently paying the monthly premium I, not only don't enough to fund any significant venture, I also have made over ten times the value of that policy by investing in real estate only a few years. Because of the power of compound interest and the need for some long term investment vehicles, I keep the mutual funds and the insurance. I have learned that your investment portfolio should be diverse and contain items that you can I understand. The next time someone offered me financial advice I made sure to look at their financial situation first.

There are risks involved in investing as any venture but the benefits have consistently been rewarding to me and so many others. Isn't it time to start getting some financial benefits?

Road to Freedom

Trusted as an investment vehicle by many of the top business men and women, Real Estate provides financial stability in up or down markets. Just think, real estate is one of those things that God is not making more of. We have what we have so there will always be a need and demand for decent homes and land.

Prosperity can be yours tomorrow by starting to invest in real estate today. Investors who entered real estate 10 years ago have seen their investments double. Investors who purchased real estate 20 years ago have seen their investments triple. In fact, according to Neighborhood Scouts, real estate has continued to appreciate since 1960 and the average neighborhood has seen an 84% since 1990. Wow, I find those facts unbelievable and encouraging for all women who want to do something positive for their futures, their fortunes, and the stability of their families.

Timing is everything. That's why the time is now. I remember some opportunities that I had 5 years ago to buy some great properties at what seemed an "okay" price at the time and I can't stop kicking myself for not getting in the game earlier. There is a popular motivational speaker who says Ready, Shoot, Aim. I like that approach because we will never be truly ready until we step out there, take some chances, learn from our mistakes, and move on from there. The best thing about real estate is that your risk is limited because it is such a safe investment.

Why The Time is Now to Begin Investing in Real Estate

The time is now to begin investing because chances of success are high. If investing is a game of risk, why not participate in an activity that will yield great possibilities of success. Real Estate is a proven appreciating asset. When properly investigated and maintained, real estate will continue to increase in value over time. If you are willing to hold onto real estate for a few years, you are highly likely to experience the rewards that ownership offers.

They still aren't making more of it—When we are all dead and gone, the land will remain. It's that simple.

The earlier you start the more equity you'll build. City after city, lot after lot, neighborhood after neighborhood, there are examples of good deals that passed many people by. If you had just purchased that lot 1 year ago or invested in this neighborhood when you saw the change.

All the Knowledge you need is available-Walk through the local library or bookstore and there are numerous resources available to help you begin your real estate investing career. In addition to the tool you hold in your hands, the back of this book contains a valuable toolkit of resources that can help you with every aspect of your business. The information is out there. It's up to you to access it.

Build your Investment Portfolio—Any financial planner will tell you that your investment portfolio should be diverse and contain real estate. Typically, the portfolio they suggest will require homeownership. The next level after homeownership is owning investment real estate.

Just the Facts

If my opinion and the opinion of a ton of real estate millionaires isn't enough to convince you, just look at the numbers. The National Association of Realtors reported in 2005 that homes were selling at record prices. HUD Reported that more and more first time homebuyers enter the real estate market each year. Unfortunately, for some of these buyers, they will end up unable to make their payments and in foreclosure. A Fannie Mae report showed that because of loose lending practices, foreclosures were at a record high.

Proven to rebound in a down market, real estate remains to be one of the safest investments for beginners. Because of all this data, I know that if so many others can make this market work for them, then certainly I can too. At minimum I can eliminate financial stress, build wealth, and experience economic independence.

And that would be my hope for every woman or man I encounter. Anyone with a desire for more money and proven investment vehicle, should look at real estate investing as part of their investment portfolio. When my husband and I made more money on one real estate deal than a year's salary from my job, we knew we were definitely in the wrong business. I have had several friends and customers to share their real estate success stories with me that I'd like to share just to show how real estate can help you achieve any goal.

What About the Housing Bubble?

When Alan Greenspan retired as chair of the Federal Reserve Board, he left at the end of a booming economic era of low interest rates and a booming housing market. Analysts and pundits have been predicting a housing decline or bubble "burst" since before Greenspan left office that has yet manifested.

Articles from the Wall Street Journal to the Boston Globe are predicting a decline but have yet to show significant figures supporting their claims. In many markets where prices soared, there has been a decline in the soar but prices have yet to strike a downward curve. Many blogs and analysts predict a 10% housing correction in some areas of the country where prices were extremely out of whack.

So in a period of a slowing market or a correcting market, how do you still make money in real estate? Is it possible? Or should you choose to invest in other areas.

If purchased properly, there is still money to be made in many markets with real estate because there will continue to be foreclosures, distressed properties, and the need for affordable housing and rental housing. As long as there continues to be a need for housing, there will be a need for real estate investors.

Real Estate investors can benefit in any market by purchasing properties at below market prices. This can be done by mastering negotiation skills, learning how to purchase properties going through foreclosure, and buying properties in emerging areas.

The techniques and skills shared in this book will teach you how to make money in a market that is booming or in a market that is slower. In both markets, you can make money in real estate investing.

What's Your Dream?

Determining what your compelling vision for your life and dreams for your future will give you the motivation to continue to press forward in pursuing your real estate career. Equity has been used over and over to help others fund their dreams and can be used to fund yours as well.

Dream Job

"I was a lawyer with hopes of becoming a judge. After I didn't get a political judicial appointment, I decided to take my cause to the people and run for the judicial seat I dreamed of. In order to win the seat I knew I would have to invest big bucks and creative strategies because my opponent was independently wealthy. In addition to my fundraising efforts, I had to take out a $50,000 home equity loan on my home in order to defeat my opponent. My bid for judge was successful. I got the job of my dreams as well as a $60,000 per year pay raise. Was my home instrumental in helping me achieve my goals, you bet. The best part is that I only owned my home 3 years and had enough equity in that short period of time to get the needed equity loan."
-Prominent Judge

Debt Free

"Debt and despair kept me stressed out so I knew I needed to simplify by selling this little investment property that I owned but couldn't keep a decent tenant in. When I met with you, you told me that I could not only pay off my mortgage but with a few upgrades I could get $15,000 more than I thought. Thanks for helping me sell this property. Not only did I get from under this house, I was able to pay off all my credit card debt, finish my bachelor's degree, and improve my credit score."
-Debt Free Brother

Entrepreneur

"When we were unable to get an SBA Loan to fund our small business, we looked to real estate to infuse the cash we needed. We were able to open the first African American owned sub franchise in our city because of the sale of 2 rehabbed properties. We let our real estate business fund the build out and development of a business that gives us a steady stream of income and when it's sold will quadruple our initial investment."
-Sub Franchise Owner

Cash Flow

"I opened a new restaurant and we were struggling for several months because the city decided to complete a major construction project on the streets in front of my building. I was in a lease that I couldn't get out of so I limped along. My saving grace was the cash flow that I consistently received from 2 apartment buildings I own. Now that the construction is over, my restaurant has really taken off and during the slow time, we were able to work out many kinks. I am so thankful that I had cash flow to get me through the rough times"
-Restaurant Owner

Retirement

"10 years ago I bought 3 brick 3/3 duplexes in a stable middle class neighborhood for $60,000 each. At the time, I thought that was a lot of money so I stopped. I wish I hadn't because now each property is worth well over $160,000 and I know the value will only keep going up. Two will be paid off soon and I think I'll just keep them until retirement and let them fund my future.
-The Millionaire Next Door

I've heard so many stories like the one's above and more. To read about more success stories, visit my website at www.realestatepowerplays.com and click on Real People, Real Power. Unfortunately, for every successful person who's profited from the real estate they own, I seem to encounter at least 10 who are afraid, or lazy, or just clueless of how to infuse power into their lives.

How do we infuse this Power into our Lives? I've incorporated the following 3 philosophies in my approach to building my empire.

1. Start—No matter how small you start or how slow you move. It has always been my belief that starting is only way to begin the process of building wealth. Small steps in the right direction are certainly better than standing still or moving backwards.
   Starting is a state of mind. Before my husband became a developer he just willed it for himself. He always considered himself a developer. It occurred to me that when you envision yourself one way, you begin to act the way this per-

son acts, and you begin to see the things that they will see. By visioning you will yourself into becoming who you are destined to be.

2. Learn as You Go—I don't want to encourage anyone to make rash and foolish decisions, however, I do insist that you begin making decisions and then learn as you go. I've met so many people who are searching the market, testing the market, waiting on the right deal. Or reading book after book and researching their investments to the point where they never pull the trigger.

At some point you have to step out there and make something happen. I was just speaking with a friend who said he and his wife was looking at purchasing some land last year and this year the price has now gone up $30,000. He said he asked the developer would the price continue to rise and the developer responded "Absolutely" and predicted it would be an additional $30,000 in another year. If your gut tells you its right then it probably is.

3. Be Quick but Not in a Hurry—Move quickly on leads. Competition is fierce for great properties. We always schedule showings right away. Although I'm quick to look at a property I always take my time to look it over thoroughly and thoughtfully crunch all the numbers. Once I've decided it's a good deal and I get a good feeling, I write the offer.

Moving quickly and being decisive has saved me a lot of time and anguish over the years. Looking forward to the possibilities of the property, the neighborhood, the equity helps you to start visioning like an investor.

Common Objections

Maybe you're still not convinced and have fears. Believe me I understand. I still get scared when unexpected things happen. However, I've trained myself to look forward and not to let fear cripple me. The situation is whatever it is. At the point in time when I've got a problem, I know I have to focus on solutions and not the problem to get ahead.

There are typically many common objections to beginning the practice investing in real estate. I've heard everything from my credit is bad to this is too hard. I closely link objections with fear. Fear is simply the opposite and absence of faith. If you have made it this far, there is obviously a desire to have more in your life. That could be more freedom, more love, more authority, more money, or more options. The way I see it if God puts a thought on our heart he will only support its implementation because God is committed to helping us reach our purpose. When I first realized that about my life, I knew that getting closer to my purpose was possible. As shown in the examples above, investing in real estate is just one tool that will remove some of the financial strongholds or financial excuses that we put in the way as excuses for not becoming who we truly are.

Our authentic self is not stressed out or defeated. Our authentic self is most concerned about being about what we are really about. Have you ever been doing exactly what you knew you should be doing at a moment? Maybe it was when you held your child for the first time. Even if you underwent hours of painful labor, the moment you were in line with your purpose you seemed to forget the struggle or hurt. I believe God wants us to get to the place of authenticity and to be aligned with our purpose. Debt like fear is one of those ghosts that stand in the way of us reaching our destiny.

CHAPTER 2

Overcoming Fear

It has been said that on the other side of fear is freedom. Wow, what an empowering thought. When I think back to all my would've, could've, should've moments, I realize that fear was the ugly culprit of me stepping into my authentic self.

Most investment books that you pick up will tell you that you've got to do a ton of research, you've got to have access to a lot of money, you've got to a have construction skills to save money, and that you've got to follow lots of specific systems and "walla!" you're a successful investor. While I will not send you out to your real estate career without ample facts, knowledge, strategies, and tools, as a born again Christian, I must share with you some simple faith rules that will propel your business, give you motivation, and provide you with enough belief in yourself to make your goal of real estate investing a reality.

With so much experience, video training libraries, audio tapes, and books galore available to anyone within reach of a library, I knew lack of knowledge was not the only roadblock to success. In fact, I would contend that the biggest roadblock is lack of belief in yourself that that stops any of us from experiencing success in real estate or any venture in life.

In real estate, there are psychological fears but I've also found there are very practical fears and responsibilities that cripple our action. But if freedom is on the other side of fear, I know for sure that faith is the vehicle that moves you from fear to freedom. The awesome thing about real estate as well is that there are a ton of facts that support our faith.

Listed Below are the 7 most Common Fears and how Faith along with a couple of Facts that can get you on the road to riches.

Fear #1

I don't have enough money.

"I don't have enough money" is always an interesting excuse from people who don't have anything. One would think if money were what you wanted and money is what you lack that you would be about finding a solution to the problem versus using the problem as an excuse for not finding a solution.

Faith: "I have all I need"

A significant bible verse on this issue of lack is listed below:

"Instruct those who are rich in this present world not to be conceited or to fix their hope on the uncertainty of riches, but on God, who richly supplies us with all things to enjoy. Instruct them to do good, to be rich in good works, to be generous and ready to share, storing up for themselves the treasure of a good foundation for the future, so that they may take hold of that which is life indeed."

1 Timothy 6:17-19

Fact: According to a recent article in USA Today, 43% of first time home buyers in 2005 purchased a new home with no money down.

Whether you're a person who looks at her bank accounts and does not see the money or not be able to make our rent let alone think about making a mortgage payment. Or maybe you're pretty successful on the outside but have no real wealth. Suze Orman calls you the Young Fabulous and Broke and don't know how to be anything else. There is truly a solution for you. The best thing about real estate is that it's a borrowed money business. Very few people spend a lot of their own money on real estate deals. Because real estate is a tangible, valuable, asset, banks will loan money and use the property as collateral.

This makes it possible for any man to get involved in real estate. And because lenders are now so loose, there are tons of programs to help owners get financial assistance and no money down program. It's possible to get into any deal with no money down. And my reading and mastering the techniques taught to you in Power Play # 4. You'll be able to not only get your primary residence for no money down but I'll share with you techniques used by the Pro's to get investments properties for no money down as well.

So, my friend, you definitely have all you need to succeed in real estate investing if this is your only Fear.

Fear #2

My Credit is Bad

Bad credit is a reality of life for many women that I've come in contact with. Poor decisions, too much debt, and mismanagement seem to be the biggest contributors to the low credit score. Where there is a will there is a way. Conquering credit begins with knowledge and understanding how credit works and how to manage what you have.

Faith "It won't be this way always"

"O love the LORD, all you His godly ones! The LORD preserves the faithful and fully recompenses the proud doer."
Psalm 31:23

Whether your credit is good or bad, there are programs and loans that you can take advantage of. Once the core issue has been fixed, move forward in faith and God will make a way.

Fact: Any infraction on your credit report is required by law to be removed in 7 years. Even bankruptcies can be removed after 10 years. Many mortgage companies offer programs for people with challenged credit.

Loose practices in today's lending environment has led to numerous people getting loans who surely would not have qualified 10 years ago. This is great if you have credit challenges. This means you can get started today as well. But I must be honest with you that credit is important and it is something that you will have to work on if you want to get the most you can out of a career in real estate investing.

I'm hoping that bad credit is just a source of a few bad decisions or hard breaks that you've had in your life versus a life of not being responsible. Bad choices and hard breaks we can work with but character flaws are for a higher power than me. Power Play #1 addresses Credit in a big way. I've found that many people are just unsure of how credit works and what affects your score. The secret to building your credit is knowing where you stand and having everything on the table. Dealing with your credit is fixable issue and is no reason to stand in your way to you achieving your financial goals. Some of the techniques I'll share with you will not even involve getting financing from a bank. So it is possible to turn your credit situation around before anyone even runs your credit report.

So, calm your credit woes and let's start investing.

Fear #3

I don't know what I'm doing

There is a quote by Martin Fischer that puts a great spin on knowledge. "Knowledge is a process of piling up facts; wisdom lies in their simplification."

It is important to acquire education and knowledge but it is more important to exercise your inherit wisdom and gut feelings.

Faith: "I can learn and I can grow"

"And Jesus answered saying to them, "Have faith in God. Truly I say to you, whoever says to this mountain, "Be taken up and cast into the sea," and does not doubt in his heart, but believe that what he says is going to happen, it will be granted him.

Therefore I say to you, all things for which you pray and ask, believe that you have received them, and they will be granted you."
Mark 11:22-24

A trip through Barnes & Noble or your local library will reveal the abundance of resources available to you to start your investing career. If you can read you can do.

Fact: There are millions of experts in the field of construction, repair, and real estate. Many provide free estimates and advice. I can open my yellow pages and find an abundance of resources.

Mentors have a powerful ability to encourage us and to believe in us and our dreams. Unfortunately, for many of us no one took them under their wing and said "Daughter, I'm going to show you the way to happiness, wealth, love, and spiritual fulfillment" But that's okay because now you hold the ultimate guide to beginning that path of financial freedom. There is a ton that I do not know but in the back of this book, I've included a wealth of resources from the best in the business.

As we stated earlier, we have what we need. Not knowing what to do is merely a state of what you haven't been exposed to. Fortunately, with the use of the internet and a library card, we now have access to the knowledge of the smartest, riches, and most successful men and women out there. I feel honored to share my experiences in hopes to alleviate the uncertainty that so many young women may find themselves.

Not knowing is no longer a fear because all the resources are available to me.

Fear #4

This is too much and too overwhelming.

There is always a fear of not being able to handle a task or being overwhelmed. Whenever I get extremely overwhelmed, I focus really hard on completing just one project. Anyone can complete one project. Maybe it's painting a bedroom or cleaning out the garage or pulling up weeds, whatever it is, start something that you can finish. Get results and see how empowered you feel.

Faith: "God will not put on me more than I can bare"

"Yet those who wait for the LORD will gain new strength; they will mount up with wings like eagles, they will run and not get tired, they will walk and not become weary."
Isaiah 40:31

This quote says it all. Walk in faith and God will strengthen, protect and guide you through your projects.

Fact: People rehab homes, buy real estate, and sell real estate everyday. Again all the resources you need are out there waiting on you to tap into them.

Common objections to real estate investing is that this process is too much or too overwhelming or too confusing to be successful with. Not true. Don't believe me, just head downtown to your local sheriffs auction and I bet you won't find any brain surgeons or rocket scientist down there. What you will find is just a bunch of folks who figured out if I buy low and sell high I make a profit. It's pretty simple and very understandable.

What I've found is that many people get overwhelmed by the details. This guide is designed to help you tackle the most common details that may trip you up. It also will help you qualify contractors, price out jobs, and sell for the highest marketable price. Many people think real estate investing isn't for women but when you look at what it takes to be really successful, I believe women were made for this business. I just need some women to believe in themselves enough to make it happen.

Women are the queens of detail and multi-tasking. Real estate investing is no harder than the tasks we handle effectively on a daily basis.

Fear #5

I don't know how to be a landlord

People make a lot of being a landlord and it's really only a business relationship with someone who live is your house. When in doubt, treat them as you'd want to be treated. Remember when you were a tenant. What did you like? What didn't you like? Keep a clean, decent, safe environment and you're on your way to being a successful landlord.

Faith: "Being myself is good enough"

"Trust in the LORD with all your heart and do not lean on your own understanding. In all your ways acknowledge Him, and He will make your paths straight."
Proverbs 3:5-6

Landlording is truly a learned skill set. It can compliment any personality type. If you like to help people, you can be a great landlord. If you like to make money, you can be a great landlord. If you don't know what you're doing, you can still be a great landlord.

Fact: There are professional property managers available to hire for less than you think. There are professionals who will provide any service to a landlord from maintenance to rent collection.

Help is available for landlords to make the process one that is not unbearable. I know that no one when they were growing up said they wanted to be a landlord when they got older. Being a landlord is one thing that you will not be able to avoid in this business. This is about being an owner, about financial independence, and being a wealth builder. In order to get a stream of cash flow income, there has got to be someone to pay it. That is going to be a tenant.

Fear of being a landlord is basically the same as fear of being an owner or fear of being a leader. This is one fear that has to be conquered in order to be a successful investor. Being a landlord does not mean being a beer belly slum lord. I was at a conference recently and someone sneerly asked me" So, the secret to financial freedom is being a landlord." No, I don't think this is the secret but I do believe it is one of those necessary steps on your road to financial freedom if you're in real estate. Even if your goal is to primarily buy and sell, there may be a time that you may have to rent a unit to cover the bills while the property is being sold. Don't fear, Landlording is simply a means to supplying a very important need, housing. Someone's got to do it so why not you.

Included in this guide are ideas to help find the best available tenants, information on finding help to manage your properties, and options for getting cash out of your properties quickly. Also we will discuss property managers and how it is possible to not do anything but collect a monthly check because of the properties you own. Now wouldn't that be nice. No work, no responsibility, collect a check—it's possible and in Power Play #8, I'll share with you some techniques to find the best managers for your properties.

Fear #6

Contractors may rip me off

This fear is a result of a lack of knowledge. The more you learn about repair needs, costs, and what it takes to own and sell a property, the more your anxiety about contractors will cease.

Faith:
"People are inherently good and I will follow my spirit"

"This book of the law shall not depart from your mouth, but you shall meditate on it day and night, so that you may be careful to do according to all that is written in it; for then you will make your way prosperous, and then you will have success."
Joshua 1:8

Operate with integrity and find others who do the same and you will have positive results. The photographer for my wedding was a little more expensive than other photographers that I interviewed but there was a since of sincerity and high moral standards that drew me to him.

Your spirit will attract others with a similar spirit. Let your spirit guide you when hiring anyone.

Fact: Most contractors are professional, licensed, and insured. These business professionals are members of professional accreditation organizations and follow strict guidelines. I can locate these professionals easily in my town.

If you do decide that you want to be a landlord then you will be amazed at your own knowledge and personal power when it comes to maintaining your property. Much of property maintenance is common sense and if something breaks, I'll give you some very practical tips on how you can choose a contractor that you can trust. Power Play #6 will include the F.R.A.N.K. Factor for success when dealing with contractors. Also we will discuss negotiation tactics that will help you not only to get the best deals for your properties but also when dealing with contractors, vendors, and other professionals within the real estate business,

Repairs will be needed along the way but you will learn that by properly inspecting and rehabbing your properties, you can limit the number of emergency calls that you receive from tenants.

Fear #7

I don't want to ruin my credit or get in bigger financial turmoil

I recently bought a book for one quote. The quote was "It's better to regret what you have done than what you haven't done." This realization hit me so hard because I know that if it doesn't kill me it will make me stronger. The knowledge and personal power that you have when stepping out on faith is what sustains you and empowers you to try again and again.

Faith: "I will move forward when I step forward"

"This book of the law shall not depart from your mouth, but you shall meditate on it day and night, so that you may be careful to do according to all that is written in it; for then you will make your way prosperous, and then you will have success."

Joshua 1:8

Fact: Repeat this affirmation: "I am financially responsible. I am setting up my real estate career to provide financial freedom and will involve myself in acts that support this goal."

Building wealth through real estate is possible and attainable while limiting your risks. We all have read the articles warning us of ambitious investors who lost it all in a bad foreclosure deal or the landlord who couldn't keep any tenants. I am not going to say that these scenarios do not exist but there is a distinct advantage that you will have before entering the realm of real estate investing and that is the advantage of knowledge. Knowledge is definitely power in this business. The best part of the knowledge is that there are so many people who have gone out and made mistakes, myself included, who you can learn from. This business is not very hard and the strategies to be successful in it are pretty simple. Most people who find themselves in a bind are usually overzealous, irresponsible, or don't follow there gut instincts.

Pace yourself and get the knowledge needed to be successful and I have the utmost faith that you will be able to build wealth in this business. I've witnessed so many examples over the past 5 years from people a lot less intelligent than you.

"For God has not given us a spirit of fear, but of power and love and discipline."
2 Timothy 1:7

That quote alone is enough to move you into action. Fear has the power to weaken us but only if we let it. On the other side of fear is freedom so don't let fear hold you back. By utilizing the 9 power plays you have tools to crush fear. Just use them and you will realize your own strength.

Advantages of Starting Now

Starting your career in real estate investing should begin now or as soon as possible. Why because if you don't and you look back on yourself 5, 10 years from now you will kick yourself over and over. That's my advice. Start slow, start small if that makes you feel better but if you're serious start now. Why.

Housing prices will most likely continue to increase. Now that's a thought. That's great for the girl who's bought today. For the girl who buys 5 years from now that means you have lost so much time and money. I ride by properties all the time that I had opportunities to buy a few years ago that I didn't buy because I was just on another planet. If I had done so, my life would have really been changed.

You will learn as you go. By not starting now, you are cheating yourself out of years of education that can lead to a more skilled and more informed you a few years from now. What an investment in you.

Why not? The risks are low if you follow my tips and you never know what your future holds. You may need the equity in that property you're eyeing to pay for it. I know you can do it because I believe this is something anybody can do.

Why is Buying Real Estate so Easy?

Buying real estate has never been easier than right now. Mortgage rates continue to be low and even with the change over from Greenspan to Bernanke. More mortgage companies are out in the marketplace competing for our business. Local mortgage brokers, internet companies, large banks all are moving towards diverse lending portfolios to service those with varying credit scores and incomes.

Winning in real estate investing is a matter of taking a chance and getting in the game. Although many new businesses fail in the first year those statistics don't apply to real estate investors because if you're pacing yourself the advantages stack up quickly.

Top Reasons to Be Fearless For Real Estate Investors

Cash investment can be low.

To start a Curves franchise, one of the hottest franchises in the market it will take a great credit score, business savvy, and an initial franchise fee of $32,000. Although some real estate does require a down payment, there are equally and perhaps even more deals that can be required without a huge financial outlay. Real estate allows you to build your wealth by borrowing money from someone else ie. The banking industry.

Time conscious.

The average retail franchise does not allow an absentee owner and based on the retail hours and start up operations this could translate into long hours away from home and your family. I will show you how you can match your current working salary with half the hours. Many real estate investments can yield returns upwards of 20%-30% if you work it right. Overall this industry could utilize a very little of your time and labor if your structure it that way. We will cover ways to help minimize your time investment throughout the book.

Tax Benefits

Many of the tax benefits associated with owning real estate can save you thousands and thousands of dollars on taxes. Real estate allows for many legal tax deductions and benefits.

Building on the Asset—As the value of your investment increases you can borrow against that equity and uses one asset as a basis to acquire new assets.

Increases in Value

Most real estate will continue to increase in value over time. Even if you're in a slow market, if you hold on long enough eventually that property will most likely go up in value.

Flexibility by Negotiation—I love it when I see some businesses and your only way in is your own cash. Real estate allows for many flexible and creative financing sources, most that don't require your own resources.

Low Failure Rate

Many new start investors, whether they stay in the business or not have achieved success or could achieve success with their investment. By easily acquiring free information a beginning investor can find simple tools to help him be successful in this business.

A former manager of mine once stated that he liked to win and when given the choice to win or lose, he'd rather be a winner. Being a winner in business, starts with knowing the basics of real estate investing. The power plays to win are simple to learn and easy to implement. No matter where you are financially today, adopting an investor's mentality can lead you on the road to financial success.

No Salary Cap

That road to financial success is not one hindered by caps, ceilings, or maximums. Objective value is the best thing I love about real estate. This is another huge advantage of starting now. The faster you begin, the faster you can achieve financial independence. And even if the value were subjective, wouldn't you prefer to purchase a property from a woman. Someone who's evaluated the neighborhood based on her standards and values, one who's taken time to handle the small details, one who's given the property her special touch.

Equity doesn't care if you're a man or a woman. There is no salary cap on the equity you can acquire for yourself through your ownership in properties. It is my theory that women have the ability to earn more because of there ability to make a house a home for a prospective buyer. And if you can make a house feel like a home for a buyer so much so that they are willing to pay whatever they can afford—That my dear is the secret to success in this business.

CHAPTER 3

Learning the Plays
Real Estate Investing for Women in a Nutshell

I've bought my own house, I have a job so
So now your ready-What to do? Make the Plays

Starting is the best way to learn the plays of real estate investing. One of my favorite advice slogans that I've heard lately was Ready, Fire, Aim. If we waited until all our ducks were in a row we might not ever get into anything new, exciting, or interesting. Real estate is one of those great acquisitions that can help you build as you move along and offers a great educational opportunity for the next project or endeavor.

Ready or not, the opportunity time is now so you might as well get started. The steps are not complicated. This book is about the basics. So many of us could change our life today just by following a few simple, basic, processes. I think we would see that we will grow into the person we want to be.

You start at the Beginning with the intangibles of the Pre-Purchase Process. This process we discussed in length in Power Play number one. Truly attitude can determine our altitude and I believe that so many people never reach their potential because they don't believe that they can do it. That's the intangible.

Power Play # 1
Get In Shape: Flex Your Credit Muscle

The tangible is simple as well. You've got to take care of some of the basics. The basics include having a job, having decent credit, and controlled debt. That's not to say that there isn't a solution for you if you have issues with any of the above but the reality is that you need to have some type of income before anyone will give you a loan. Although it's certainly possible to enter in lease options or rent to own but no matter what type of financing you get, you've got to make a payment or creatively find someone to make a payment for you. Since you bought this book or checked it out in the library, we'll assume you have some type of income because I do not want you so stretched out trying to make a payment you can't afford that you end up making your situation even worse.

Secondly you need to have some control over your debt. Well, Latisha, that's why I'm reading this book. I simply mean that ideally you want a debt to income situation that will give you an opportunity to secure mortgages and loans.

Finally, a decent credit score would be helpful. If you've got credit issues we'll discuss those at length later and I'll give you some painless tips for cleaning up your credit quickly.

Power Play 2
Know the Players: Your Real Estate Success Team

Mortgage brokers, realtors, and other Pre-Purchase Advisors can provide a great value but can also be discouraging at time. My advice is to pick some advisors who work with buyers like you. When you pick a realtor, make sure it's someone who spends part or all of her time working with investors. Pick a lender who is comfortable and experienced with creative loan strategies. They all would rather have a cookie cutter buyer because that means they get paid faster. But there are agents and loan officers out there who are now specializing in budding investors like you because they realize the repeat business and value what you are doing.

So once you've selected these people, Go meet with them. What do they require? Tell them what your goals are. I'd recommend being honest and then you will know right away if they can help you. Most will pre-qualify you and tell you what you need to do to get to your goals.

Power Play #3
You Don't Have to Pay to Play
Using Other People's Money

The sheer beauty of investing in real estate is the ability to build wealth by using someone else's money. In real estate, your collateral for getting the loan is the real estate you purchase but the equity you build is yours. Leveraging this great American process is your greatest tool with building a real estate empire. In order to leverage this properly, you need to be in the strongest financial position you can be in first. This includes having an excellent credit score, building your savings, and shopping around for the best deal.

If you've already met with a mortgage banker early in the process and even though he's given you some options you want to look for your own. Look for motivated seller and sellers in situations that may motivate them to offer assistance and be willing to negotiate so you can get your property at a wholesale price.

Your ultimate goal is buy your investment properties with other people's money. There have been many books written about buying with nothing down and many are great. I've compiled for your some ideas that I think are the best and ones that have personally worked for me. These are easy techniques any one can do.

Power Play#4
Buying with No Money Down

The sister to using other people's money is buying with no money down. If you know you are going to be buying smart and building equity on someone else's resources, it only make sense to do this without using any of your money if you can.

Many finance books and brokers will tell you not to buy a home until you can afford some of the down payment and they may be right but you are now thinking as an investor and you should think strategically and make good buying decisions. Once you've made a good buying decision, then we will negotiate to get you the best deal ever.

And the best deal ever is not only buying using someone else's money but to do it in such a way where you have no money out of pocket and possibly even the resources to help you repair the property and re sell it for a profit.

In this power play we will look at strategies the pro's use to buy real estate using no money down.

Power Play #5
Starting small

I know many beginning investors want to buy a diamond in the ruff fore-closure from some little old lady that requires little work and can be sold for a huge profit. Well, I hate to disappoint you, in today's world the competition to buy foreclosures in fierce. Many times you will also find yourself competing with investors who have a lot of cash and experience. But that's not to discourage you. You can do it. I know you can. You've just got to consistently shop and be ready to act when you encounter the prime situation.

There's nothing wrong with starting small. I've found that with most of my clients one or two deals can change the direction of their life. That's amazing! What if in 3-6 months you could be on a path to wealth and prosperity. Would your current job give you that opportunity?

Our strategies in this power play will focus on starting small and moving strategically. We will begin by focusing on the merits of the single family home and buying a safe, tried and true investment.

Power Play #6
Understanding Foreclosures: The Play by Play

In power play number 6, we will look at buying foreclosures and how to avoid many of the pitfalls you've probably read about or heard about. There are many myths that surround buying foreclosures. In Power Play number 6, we will dispel the myths of buying foreclosures.

Foreclosures can be fun. Yes I said it. They can also be some of the scariest financial encounters you find yourself in if you don't do it right.

Power Play #7
Rehabbing for Riches

With Foreclosure you have to also look at Rehabbing and Flippers. Flipping just means buying, rehabbing, and re-selling. We are not talking about illegal scams but bonafide upgrades and good business decisions. There will be times that you want to hang on to properties and other times when the property is prime for selling off or flipping.

Many investors got themselves in trouble in the late 90's with getting involved in illegal practices using home values, appraisers, and inflated pricing. We will only be offering sound real estate advice and promoting legal and ethical dealings.

There is nothing to be ashamed of if you make a smart business decision and re-sell a property for a profit. Most real estate investors provide a great public service because the average homebuyer does not want to put in the sweat equity to build a house up from ugly to unforgettable. So be proud of what you do and realize that your hard work and foresight has created a win/win for the buyer, the neighbors, the neighborhood, yourself, and so much more.

Power Play #8
Rental Properties

In Power play #8, we will look at rentals and landlording. Face it, eventually; you're going to have to do it. But I promise it doesn't have to be painful if you follow some simple steps for pre-screening tenants, using property managers, and buying in the right neighborhoods.

Rentals can be intimidating, a head ache, and stressful but they can also be your biggest long-term gold mine.

We will explore rental properties and how they fit into your wealth creation plan.

Power Play #9
Play to Win: Playing Smart with Taxes and Exchanges

I promise you that you will make mistakes along the way but the mistakes will only make you stronger and more knowledgeable for the next deal. Power play nine will also show you how to use attorneys, realtors, accountants, and other resources to make your business soar and overcoming the biggest financial hurdle, taxes. We will look at playing smart with smart people.

We will explore getting your personal and outside resources in order. So join us through the next nine power plays for success in any market. With intelligence and lack of fear, you can accomplish any goals that you set out to achieve.

Part Two

9 POWER PLAYS FOR SUCCESS

POWER PLAY#1

Get In Shape—Flex Your Credit Muscle

Professional athletes know that in order for them to compete in their chosen sport that they have to be in shape. The same theory could apply for becoming a successful real estate investor. The best part about being in shape for real estate investing is that 90 percent of the population could play if they chose to. Our great country allows most individuals the ability to purchase a home. In 2004, 70% of the nation owned a home and I know that there are many others who are able to own a home if they focused on making it happens.

So how do you get into shape? Getting in shape is a process of being mentally fit and financially fit. Being mentally fit is making a decision and believing you can accomplish it. Being financially fit is simply having a job or steady stream of income and having a credit score to support the loans you'll be getting. A strong credit muscle gives you more strength and flexibility in the real estate game. It's as simple as that.

Since 95% of you already have a job or stream of income, I will focus on getting your credit score as high as possible. Although we will discuss many options throughout the book that may not require you to have the best credit, Good credit is always a positive because it will give you more options and control.

Your Credit Objective = Score high to Win

Ask a lender, credit bureaus, or FICO himself and no one will give you a clear answer on how credit bureaus get your exact credit score. FICO is an acronym for Fair Isaac Corp. and they are a Minneapolis based company that has created a risk calculation formula that determines an individual's default risk. This risk is based on late payments, number of credit inquiries, percentage of credit limit usage and delinquencies. FICO scores range from 300-850 and the higher the score the better.

The average credit score at the time of print was 676 for all borrowers. Good credit is usually anything 700 and up. Needs improvement scores are about 600 and below.

Not only in real estate loans but these days more and more entities are reviewing credit scores to make decisions. Landlords will use the credit score before renting, employers will check your score to determine your level of responsibility, and even some insurance companies will use your credit score to determine your insurability. Getting your credit as high as possible and keeping it that way, will prove to give you benefits in your real estate business and in many other life transactions.

Where do I start?

Understanding where you are is the most important part of controlling your credit 'ability.' Pulling your credit report has never been easier because the major bureaus are all online. The following is the contact information for finding your credit report.

Equifax
www.equifax.com
Equifax Credit Information Services, Inc
P.O. Box 740241
Atlanta, GA 30374
1-888-685-1111

Transition
www.transunion.com
TransUnion
Post Office Box 2000
Chester, PA 19022
1-800-916-8800

Experian
www.experian.com
1-888-397-3742

Your credit report can be obtained from each bureau for around $9. Some states will allow a free copy of your credit report if you've been denied for a loan. My favorite report is a 3 in 1 report that also gives you your credit score. These are usually about $30 but the information in the report is invaluable and will greatly assist you on your road to Great Credit. Also, the reports are available instantly online. If you haven't ordered a 3 in 1 lately, at the end of this chapter is a great time to pull the report and learn where you stand.

Each of the companies' websites also provides helpful information for how you can improve your scores and how to dispute mistakes on your report.

What's in Your Report?

Each of the credit bureaus are pretty much the same as far as the information they collect on you. Occasionally, you may find that one company may carry a debt or creditor that is missing on one of the others. This is why many lenders have moved to 3 in 1 reports as well. And although each report may vary slightly, they will take an average of the 3 reports to determine your credit score.

Your report will contain personal and historical information about you and your debts. Personal Information such as name, address will be included on all 3 reports. Any name changes or variations of your name will also be included.

History of Credit is the heart of the credit report and will contain each creditor that you have had and the length of time you've had an open account with this company. It will also contain payment data and whether the debt is revolving or fixed. This section will also have your payment amount

Inquiries are another consistent and important part of the report. This section will show you every company that has requested a copy of your credit report. The number of inquiries can affect your score if there are too many inquiries in a short amount of time.

Public Information will include any judgments, liens, or delinquencies that have been recorded against you.

The data on your credit report will stay for 7 years so determining the accuracy is critical to your credit success.

I've Got It—Now What?

Once you've pulled your credit report, I would search for accuracy and disparaging marks. Look through the entire report with a highlighter and anything that is not correct should be highlighted. These could be as simple as accounts that are show they are open that you closed years ago to a previous mortgage that should have been paid off that is still active.

The worst of the bad marks are delinquencies, collections, or a bankruptcy. Those delinquencies must be settled before you can qualify for most loans. Depending on the age, they may also be settled directly with the collection agency or lender. Any mistakes should be disputed right away because they can be removed.

To dispute an error, you must write the credit bureau a letter explaining the discrepancy. Each site contains a simple online investigation form that you can use to advise them of errors. After you alert the credit bureau of the mistake, the credit bureau will investigate the charge directly with the source and verify its accuracy. It is important to check each individual bureau to see if the information is incorrect with each agency. You must submit a separate letter to each credit agency to dispute a mistake. The agency is required by law to follow up with you on the outcome of their investigation.

If the credit bureau cannot verify the charge, then that mistake should be removed from your credit report. This whole process takes a minimum of 30 days and up to 60 days. To have an incorrect item removed you should contact both the company that has reported the information incorrectly as well as each credit bureau that has the information.

Understanding your Score

Your credit score is a compilation of all the information you find on your report quantified by a number. It can be as low as 350 and as high as 800; This number basically gives a creditor a probability based on pass performance of your likelihood to pay.

Your credit score is determined by a variety of factors pre-determined by Fair Isaacs Corporation or FICO. Fair Isaacs is the standard used by banks and other crediting agencies. According to information available from Fair Isaacs, they use 5 factors to determine your credit score.

1.Payment History—35%

Paying your bills on time has a significant impact on how high your credit score will be. Companies will report to the credit bureau on a consistent basis whether or not you made your payment on time or if it was 30, 60, 90, or more days overdue. If your payment is made before it is 30 days overdue it is still considered 'on time' as far as credit scoring goes but once it is into the next month, you can receive a ding for a late payment. A few late payments on your report don't rule out an overall good report if the late payments are not consistent.

2. Debt Percentage?—30%

Understanding how the amount of debt you carry affects your score has always been a little vague and confusing for me. Because your score doesn't consider how much income you earn, it didn't seem to make sense that the amount of debt you carry should affect your score.

The way that they determine if your debt percentage is too high is by considering your credit limits on your credit cards for example. Do you have numerous credit cards that are maxed out?

Also, if you owe lots of money on lots of accounts, the probability that you may be late on a payment increases.

3. Length of Credit—15%

The longer you've had credit, the better your FICO score will be. Having a consistent and lengthy credit history shows a lender that you have responsibly managed your credit over a period of time.

This is why that it is good to keep good accounts open to build up your credit.

4. Number of New Accounts—10%

Having many new credit accounts especially during a concentrated period of time can lower your score, because FICO considers you a higher risk especially, if you don't have a seasoned credit history. FICO scores do take into consideration shopping for a lower interest rate. Usually the score does not associate higher risk with shopping for a better rate.

5. Variety of Credit—10%

Having a variety of credit types can balance out your credit report and affect your score. Credit cards, retail accounts, installment loans, and mortgage loans, etc. represent most of the types of accounts that will appear on a credit report. Having a balanced mix will improve your score but it's not necessary to have all categories. This can be a problem if all your debt is tied up into one are like finance companies or credit cards.

What does not affect your score?

Lenders will look at your total financial picture to make a credit decision and not just your report. Your credit score does not include many important factors that factor into a lenders decision. These factors include your income, employment history, and the type of credit you're requesting. None of these factors are included in your score. FICO scores do not include your own inquiries so you can feel comfortable staying on top of your own credit score and report accuracy.

One interesting thing that I learned at a credit workshop was that your credit score is a snapshot in time. So, if your debt percentage is very high at one moment you are not doomed to have that score for a period of time. If you pay down all your debts and lower that debt percentage and, as long as that information is reported, you could have a totally different score on the next pull because the calculations are now different. There are also other tips and tricks that I've learned across the years that can help you to improve your score quickly.

7 Steps to Improve Your Credit Score Quickly

1. Know where you stand. Pull a report.

I cannot stress enough the premise of "Know Thyself." Knowing yourself gives you perspective. Knowing yourself gives you a baseline. Knowing yourself gives you an awesome opportunity to improve yourself. So as it relates to Credit, you must know where you stand. You should be keenly aware of every debt listed on your report and its accuracy. It amazes me how so many people are embarrassed by their own credit report. At this point it is what it is so look at it and I promise you can deal with it.

If you've got a 6 month old report and you've made some positive moves, then it's time for a new report. As I stated earlier, pulling your own credit report does not adversely affect your score so go for it.

You do not want to go visit a lender and be surprised by what he will tell you. Knowledge is power and if you have some credit issues, why not tackle them in the privacy of your own home versus having some unknown banker discourage you.

2. Check for accuracy. Dispute what's not correct

According to a July 2004 report by the U.S. Public Interest Research Group, 25% of credit reports had errors. Many of these errors were enough to get denied a loan. There are so many possibilities for error especially if you have multiple credit accounts.

And now with identity theft and the use of technology, it's always possible that something is incorrect on your report.

I thought identity theft was just a big urban legend for a while but more and more I meet people who've had to spend years fighting through identity theft.

Also depending on your creditors you don't know how they may report your information. My grandmother and aunt (by marriage) had the exact same name and used the same bank in a small town and were constantly in disputes. Don't trust their information. Trust only what you know is true.

I've found mistakes on my own report often and these small mistakes can and most likely will affect your score.

Dispute the items with the credit bureau. Also, I would contact the source as well because the credit bureau may want to see that you've attempted to resolve the matter directly with the creditor. It's your credit, protect it.

3. Types of Debt Prioritize pay off (negotiate any judgments, collections)

If you have a high amount of debt, that doesn't mean your credit score will be low if you manage it okay. The quickest way to improve your score is to negotiate and pay off all negative judgments or collections.

Secondly, you must reduce the amount owed on credit cards. As stated earlier, credit card debt is measured by the credit limit divided by the amount owed. It is better to have 2 $1000 limit credit cards with only $500 of debt owed versus 1 $1000 limit card that is maxed out.

4. Become fanatic About Paying on Time

A positive payment history is 35% of your credit score and the highest contributor to your credit score. Become fanatic about paying your bills on time. Pay online or sign up for automatic pay or whatever it takes to make those payments on time. Some of us control freaks don't like the idea of others drafting our accounts but it can be a lifesaver for your credit.

By consistently paying on time and showing a positive trend of on time payments you can reverse many negative trends over time. You always want to look better, more stable, and more responsible today than you did in the past. And we can all benefit from this tip.

5. Don't open new accounts

To open a new account you must apply for credit and they will pull a credit report. This will affect you negatively in 2 ways; first by having an additional credit inquiry and then by having a new account without an established credit history. Avoid this problem by not opening any new accounts.

I've met people who have a credit card with a great credit limit but will open a new card because of a rate. Don't do that. Get your credit score up and then call your credit card company and request a rate reduction.

Most credit card companies have rules for qualifying for a rate reduction. If you pay on time consistently for a year, you may qualify for a rate reduction. That's another reason why direct payments are great as well.

6. Don't Close Old Accounts

Don't close your old accounts because they may add some "season-ability" to your credit. Make the old accounts work for you by leveraging your membership history and your years of being a good customer. Banks like to see that you have been responsible over a long period of time.

Showing a positive long term history may supersede some of the negative "hick up" marks that could appear in your report. If you need more credit, you may be able to use your time with the company to request a credit line increase. This could give you higher unsecured credit line for your future real estate purchases. Also, another use for this higher credit line is to transfer balances over for a discounted rate.

7. Consolidate Bills

These transfer balances can help consolidate your debt. Using your old accounts to consolidate and get low balance transfer rates can simplify your debts. There is no use in having 4 credit cards with $500 of debt on them if you've got one with a $5000 limit. You may be able to negotiate a balance transfer rate that's lower than your other rates and still preserve your score because the balance is less than half the credit limit on your $5000 card. This also helps you lower your payments, simplify your billing, and improve your credit score.

The steps I outlined above can be accomplished by anyone on their own. There are companies who claim to help you "fix" your credit or agencies that provide free credit counseling. They may be helpful to you if you have extenuating circumstances such as identity theft or a series of judgments. For the average person, I believe you can do it yourself and do it quickly.

One of the easiest things you can do to begin to be successful in real estate investing is to be prepared. Having a good credit score gives you many more options. This is Power Play number one because credit needs to be dealt with so you can move on to all the fun stuff we'll discuss later. And it's important to know that bad credit won't kill you in real estate.

Do I Need Great Credit to Invest in Real Estate?

In real estate investing, having a high score just makes your life easier but I would not let a poor score stop me from moving forward. There are lenders all over that may give you a loan without having a high credit score. My advice, work on your credit because it will help you but continue with your real estate deals to achieve financial independence.

I've seen people who once had poor credit save themselves from their low credit scores and high debt ratios with one real estate deal. Making a cash profit of thousands of dollars and having the ability to pay down debt, may just be what your credit score needs.

In Power Play 2 we will discuss the players in that will assist you with building your real estate empire. We will look a realtors and what value they bring, lenders and the variety of programs they can offer and sellers and ways to get seller financing.

POWER PLAY #2

Know the Players: Your Real Estate Success Team

Someone told me once that a real estate deal is touched by 64 people before it closes. Wow that's 64 potential people to pass on their judgments, biases, and mistakes onto your deal. That's 64 people who could help you or hurt you in making the deal one that is smooth and manageable.

Power Play number 2 will focus on the 15 people who make your deal happen and the Big 3 players in a deal who can make your deals smooth and reachable.

The Big 3 in this list of 15 are the Seller, The Lender, and The Real Estate Agent and they all have different motivations that you must understand in order to adequately interact with each of them.

The BIG 3

The Seller

Motivations of the seller play a key role in how you as a buyer and investor should interact with them. A person may decide to sell a property for a variety of reasons. They could have the need to sell because of a death, divorce, relocation, job loss, or other life change. They could also be selling because of downsizing, need for money, cashing out, foreclosure, or more. The important thing to know is because there are many different reasons that the owner is selling his property his motivations may also be different for each situation.

Many buyers have misconceptions that all sellers just want the highest price they can get when in actuality some sellers may want a buyer who can close by a certain date. Some may want a buyer that has cash because something may prevent a mortgage from going through smoothly. Some want a buyer who is willing to accept a property as is versus one that would want the seller to complete numerous repairs.

Because sellers have different motivations, it is important to find out the answers to the following questions:
Why are you selling?
What's your price?
How long have you lived here?
How much do you owe?
What's your move out or closing date goal?
Are you willing to offer financing?

Listen to the seller's answers to determine his level of motivation to sell the property. While listening to the seller's needs and desires, always look for a win/win. If you meet the seller's time goals can he meet your wholesale pricing goals? If you meet the seller's price, will he carry a second mortgage for you? Finding a win/win begins with give and give. One of the best parts of real estate is that in a deal everyone has the potential to win and achieve their goals. By having this as your goal, you should be able to have more successful offers.

Classify your seller
How do I classify a seller?

Hot—Highly motivated
Warm—Negotiable
Cold—Not flexible

The Lender

Find a lender who is helpful and able to help you achieve your goals. When evaluating your bank or loan officer, you want to be sure that they will be able to secure programs that are in line with your goals. For example, many lenders may prefer to do a refinance because its easy money and some may shy away from foreclosure sales because the deal has a tendency to be a little more complicated. But believe me there are plenty of people out there who want your business and will help you meet your goals.

Beware of the lenders, realtors, or others in the process that tries to discourage you. Based on my experience as a real estate agent, investor, and young woman, there will be many people who may not believe that what you are trying to make happen can happen. And it's not because they have not seen it happen before or because they don't know how to help you facilitate the process of making it happen but they simply may have some preconceived notions of your skills and abilities to handle an investment real estate undertaking.

So, why would they think this? I would venture to say that although they are in the business they may have not actually been involved in their own personal real estate investments in the past or the present. Second, they may have seen people who were unprepared or overzealous get involved in a careless or foolish deal. Third, they may look at the various costs and processes involved in rehabbing a home as overwhelming. My advice is to surround you with people who support your goals and aspirations. Surround yourself with advisors who help you see how you can make something happen versus why you can't make it happen. We already know you can make it happen because many people do it everyday. We need to know how you can circumvent any obstacles so you can get to your goals more quickly and more effectively.

So what do I do?

Get good advisors, Get resourceful advisors, Get open-minded advisors… Always ask how and what would I need to do this?

Truth will be uncovered when you first meet with your lender. He or she should let you know yes you can get the loan, no you can't and here's why, or most often, if you get or have this, then I can give you a loan. I always recommend you meet with a lender first because I believe the easiest way to get started in real estate investing is the realm of the known. The realm of the known will give you your most advisors, your most options, and your most protections.

Getting approved by a lender is 1st basic step in buying a home. Buying an investment property is not much different. You want to buy your property using a loan because it's borrowed wealth building. Basically, you have an opportunity to build equity, increase your cash flow income, and improve the quality of your financial life on someone else's money. This is the ideal situation. If you had thousands of dollars sitting around and wanted to get into real estate investing, why spend your money when you can leverage your good credit and your good job into a loan secured by the real estate. This is the great wealth building strategy of real estate. Just invest a portion of it and continue to maximize those returns.

What Happens at a lender?

Whether you decide to use your local bank, a mortgage broker or an internet lender they all will request similar information from you.

Some of the items that you will need to qualify for a mortgage are as follows:
1. A Job or source of steady income
2. 2 years of W2 or taxes
3. Checking and Savings Account Statements
4. Source of Down Payment
5. Assets in 401K, stocks or insurance
6. Credit Report—Credit score over 650 ideal

Don't be discouraged if you don't have all of those items listed above. Throughout this book, we will discuss creative ways to obtain financing and non traditional funding sources that don't require all of the above information.

In the past the only way to get a mortgage was going to a bank or mortgage company and meeting with a loan officer face to face in your richest, smartest looking outfit to try to get a loan. Today with call centers and the internet all of this has changed.

With companies like Lending Tree, you can apply online using one form and get multiple options. Using an internet lender could be great if you know what you're doing and know what you need to work on or if you have excellent credit and credentials and just need a loan.

Some of the Advantages of Faceless Lender:

Why would I want to use a Faceless Lender?

Advantages

They are quick—you can do it from your phone or computer and usually get instant results or same day decisions

They are simple-It's usually a quick online application or telephone application. They don't need to see all your statements and check stubs up front. The application is contingent upon all the information you provided being verified

They are impartial-The decisions made by these companies are based solely on numbers. They feed your information into the computer and it spits out a response

Disadvantages

May be less able to make subjective decisions based on your unique situations. Local lenders or appraisers may be more aware of the area and may be able to make local decisions and recommendations that a lender 1000 miles away can't see.

May be a little more cumbersome to close the deal because of beaurocracy and lack of empowerment. Sometimes online lenders may have a call center outside of the US where the agent's sole job is to handle one part of your transaction. This especially becomes a problem if you need to move up a closing date or get a quick answer. I've even experienced language barriers that have been quite frustrating.

No personal contact or follow up because of the volume of deals each loan officer has.

How can Mortgage Brokers help me with my real estate needs?

Mortgage brokers can be helpful in obtaining your real estate loans but I would not look at them as the only resource. The advantage of working with a mortgage broker is that they typically have a lot of flexibility in finding loan programs that meet your needs. A mortgage broker usually works with a variety of lenders that all have different programs. Some lender will have more competitive programs designed for investors while some will not. A good mortgage broker should be able to provide you with several options to help fund your mortgage.

If your credit is not up to par then a mortgage broker is more likely to have a relationship with a lender that makes riskier loans than a traditional bank. If you are not going to owner occupy a property the bank already considers you a high risk and then if you have bad credit then you classified an even higher risk.

Fees from mortgage brokers tend to be higher than the traditional bank. Mortgage brokers are paid on the origination fees and points charged to the buyer in your closing costs. Mortgage brokers also aren't aware of all the fees that a lender may charge in order to close the loan. I've also found that mortgage brokers have less control over when a loan closes and they are unable to make decisions in house. Mortgage brokers can be good in some cases but remember that they are not your only option for obtaining your mortgage loan.

Small Local Banks

Your local banker could become your best partner in financing your real estate deals. Local banks may be one bank or a few local branches in your area. They may hold 20-50 million in deposits and provide a comprehensive line of mortgage loans. Local banks usually have decision making ability in house and may be able to match or beat rates or closing costs quoted by larger lenders or mortgage brokers. The first place to start with a local bank is the one that you have your account with. I've found that local banks will be less likely to work with you if they do not hold you're checking and savings accounts. They take it personally that you are seeking a loan from them but do not trust your money and deposits with them.

If you have your account with a local bank, it is worth your time to schedule a meeting with the loan officer.

Traditional Lenders

These are the big banks that focus on full service banking and mortgages. They are usually regional and may be national. They are large and impersonal. Many of their mortgage operations have moved to call centers and specialized offices. They typically deal with conventional loans and want to make safe and uncomplicated loans. Few of these lenders specialize in sub prime lending or non conventional loans. If you have good credit and a solid job history, however, working with these lenders can save you hundreds or thousands of dollars on closing costs, fees, and interest rates. These lenders usually have the same advantages of the Faceless Lender with an added benefit of a local office where on sight decisions can be made if necessary.

Throughout your investment career, you will encounter several of these types of lenders based on the type of loan you are in need of for your properties. In all cases having a great credit rating, assets, and proof of income will improve your ability to get flexible loans that meet your needs. Find a good lender that knows you and your situation and financing your deals could be a seamless process.

The Real Estate Agent

The next person that you will encounter in the real estate process and sometimes the first person is the real estate agent. Most investors will agree that a real estate agent is an asset on your team; however, you may encounter investors who prefer to go at it alone. There are both advantages and disadvantages for having a realtor help you. While starting your investment career, this person could be your best ally.

6 Advantages for Working with a Real Estate Agent

1. Access to MLS and Listings

The biggest advantage of obtaining a realtor is her access to the MLS and listings. Realtors have up to the minute data about properties that have hit the market so you can find properties more quickly. By sharing with your realtor your ideal property type, area, and price they can do searches to make your hunt a lot easier. Most agents should be able to set up your search criteria in their computer system so that you are emailed those listings automatically as they become available. Being the first to discover a property is a huge advantage of buying properties because great deals don't stay around long. Remember there are numerous other investors out there that may be looking for the same deal you're looking for.

You'll also find as you venture into certain types of investments such as city foreclosures, HUD, or VA foreclosures that the only way to access those properties is through a licensed real estate agent. For example in the city of Milwaukee, City Foreclosures will only accept offers from licensed agents. For these reasons, it is always nice to have a real estate agent on your side for these types of deals.

2. Information on Market

Realtors also have access to information on the Market. They can see how quickly houses are selling in an area, prices of home sales, and specifications on the properties. Using a Realtors Comparative Market Analysis can help you to identify trends in the area and make better offers.

It is important to understand as much as possible about your investment market and area. If you have a realtor that you work with who understands the market conditions, this can save and make you tons of money. It should be your goal to learn as much as you can about the market so that you are as knowledgeable as this person, however, until you do you can lean on their expertise until you have have market experience.

3. Information on Processes

Agents are a great resource on how the entire real estate process works. This is all they do so having one on board should help the offer and closing process flow more smoothly. The agent will typically serve as an intercessory to other real estate agents, the seller, the title company and others involved in the process. Your agent can take care of administrative matters that you may be unfamiliar with or don't want to handle.

4. Connection With Other Real Estate Professionals

Because real estate is their primary source of income, real estate agents are tied into other real estate professionals in the city. They can usually provide a list of good home inspectors, appraisers, lenders, or others that you may need in your transaction. For a beginner, you will need referrals to other professionals in the real estate arena to help your deals to flow.

5. No Cost to Buyer

Buyer's agents are available to an investor at no cost. Typically, the seller will pay the real estate broker fees. When a house is listed on the market there is an upfront agreement with the seller and the listing agent on a commission to be paid at closing out of the sellers fees. So, if a house is say 100,000 and the listing commission is 6%, the seller will pay the $6000 to the listing broker. As a part of the MLS agreement between the listing agent and your buyers agent they will split this $6000 some how. It could be 3% and 3% or 4% and 2%. Whatever the agreement in this scenario, you don't have to personally pay this fee. Most traditional purchases will fall within the above fee structure.

Watch out for discount brokers and split fee brokers, however. There are all sorts of fee arrangements that may be made with the seller by some of these small brokers. If the seller is using a discount broker, they may not be offering a commission to the buyer's broker so this is a fee you may have to negotiate in your offer to purchase. Your real estate agent should be aware of this before writing an offer and can discuss payment options with you.

If you are in a signed buyer's agent agreement with the broker, they may hold you accountable for the commission in a no fee deal or for sale by owner deal if they write up the offers for you. Before you work with an agent, you should find out upfront what fees they will charge.

6. Helpful finding Deals

A great agent can be really helpful in finding deals for you. They may be aware of listings not on the market yet or may know owners of multiple properties that they can refer deals over to you. Agents also become aware of deals that have fell through. They can also help point out emerging markets or properties that may be hidden gems.

Having a real estate agent on board is typically to your advantage; however, there are a few disadvantages that you should keep your eye out for.

What are the 6 Disadvantages of Working with a Real Estate Agent?

1. Not Investors

Although intimately involved in many real estate deals, you will encounter many real estate agents that are not investors. They are interested in putting together deals, making their commission, and moving on. Because of this they will not think like you think.

2. Prefer Traditional buyers and Sellers

Many agents prefer traditional buyers and sellers who are looking for or selling a primary residence. These buyers are typically more motivated. They are motivated by emotion such as a need to relocate their family to a new city or a need to sell their home so they purchase their new home. A typical buyer may be emotionally tied to a certain neighborhood or school district because it benefits them personally. This emotion is much different from that of an investor who is looking at the numbers of the deal and how quickly a neighborhood is appreciating.

3. Not Creative

If an agent doesn't have experience working with investors, they may not be familiar with the numerous creative verbiage that can be added to an offer. If your agent is writing the offer for you, you must be certain that they are adding the language you prefer in the offer to protect your rights.

Most will add the most common contingencies such as financing or home inspection but may not add additional contingencies that you may find necessary to add.

4. Not Patient

Buying a home is usually an emotional purchase for most buyers. As an investor, you have to learn to buy based on the numbers, potential, criteria of the property. Because an investor is in search of good deal, it may take walking through numerous properties first to find that deal. In fact, I would encourage you to not rush into a purchase if the numbers don't add up.

Many agents may not have time to accompany you on showing after showing of properties that you are not going to buy. This lack of patience will make some real estate agents prefer not to work with you.

5. Commissions

When selling your properties, real estate agents usually charge a hefty fee to list and market your home. Fees can range from 5-7% of the sales price. Some fees may be negotiable if you're sending a lot of business your agent's way. There are usually many advantages for letting a real estate professional market your property when you're ready to sell. The property will sell faster and real estate agents are tied into buyers and other agent's customers.

It's key to keep in mind these prices when determining the actual equity in a home and profits from your sales prices.

6. Extra Person

For every extra person involved in your transactions, there is almost always an extra fee. Real estate agents bring a lot of value and expertise but it is not free.

Some Questions to ask your Real Estate Agent

Have you worked with investors before?
Can you set me up to receive automatic listings?
What are your commissions and fees?
What markets seem to have the most potential?

How much time do you have to show me properties?
Are you connected to lenders that specialize in working with investors?
Does your company receive bank REO listings?
Do you work as a buyer's agent or seller's agent?
Do you require a buyer agency agreement?

Should I become my own real estate agent?

It is not necessary for you to be a real estate agent to invest in real estate but I don't think it's a bad idea. I begin my real estate career as an agent and then moved to an investor. If I had not seen the good and bad of investing first, I don't know if I would have had the guts to begin investing in real estate.

Some of the advantages of becoming your own agent:

Have your own access to the MLS
Easier access to Comparable Market Analysis and other tools
Can get into listings easier
Independence to handle own deals
Can receive commission on your own deals
Can receive additional income stream by helping others find deals
Can become a broker and hire other agents

Some things to consider:

Must attend real estate school
Must follow state's disclosure laws and agent code of ethics
May have sales requirements if you work under a broker
Must pay fees to maintain license and access to MLS

The Other 12 People You May Encounter

The Appraiser

The appraiser will typically be hired by your lender to ensure that if you get a mortgage that the house is worth the loan amount. You will typically pay the appraisers fee with your loan application or with your closing fees.

The Home Inspector

Hired by you, this inspector will give you a visual inspection and report on the condition of the home. Inspections are typically recommended unless you are a construction expert.

The Property Manager

This is a professional who manages rental property on the behalf of the owner. This person may collect rent, handle maintenance, repairs, etc. Property may charge based on a percentage of rents collected or by the services that they perform.

The Title Company

The title company will investigate title and issue a title insurance policy. Clean title is recommended and required by the lender prior to issuing a loan.

The Closing Agent

This is the person or company who handles the closing of the transaction. They will process paperwork, checks, and facilitate the exchange of keys.

The Sellers Attorney

An attorney who represents the seller's interests.

The Neighbors

Can be very helpful in understanding a property, neighborhood, and previous tenants.

The Tenants

They can give you valuable information on the property. After purchase, they are the people that will be living in your home.

The City Inspector

This inspector works for the municipality and often issues code violations or code compliance certificates. They ensure that properties are maintained at a certain level.

The City Assessor

This city official determines the taxable value of a property. It may not be the fair market value or the appraised value.

Code Compliance Officer

This officer works with the city inspector to ensure a property is habitable and determines if new standards should be set.

The Contractor

Contractors are key contributors to the repairs or upkeep of any properties that you purchase.

These are just a few of the people that will be instrumental in the ease of your real estate career. Throughout your time as an investor, you will determine who is most important and who can help you to achieve your investing goals.

In the next power play, we will spend some time looking at lenders and other people that can help you finance your investment. Financing is a key factor when you are leveraging your ability to be financed. Great financing will give you a greater opportunity to invest and build.

Power Play #3

"You don't have to Pay to Play" Using Borrowed Money to Build Wealth

Borrowing money to build your wealth is a novel concept that has been in existence since mortgages were invented. The greatest aspect of real estate investing is that you can obtain borrowed money wealth. Banks will lend you money to purchase an appreciating asset and it is secured by the asset. This very formula has made many people rich. This same formula can make you rich and work in your life. It's so simple of a concept that it is mind boggling to me why every person seeking financial independence is not into real estate.

Some are thinking that it takes money to make money. It takes good credit to get a loan. This is only a half truth. It does make it easier to make money when you have money to invest. It does make it easier to get a loan if you have good credit. This chapter is designed to show you that while it may be easier to do certain things if your situation were better, it is not impossible to achieve your goals. If you are willing to be bold, be a little creative, and put the question on the table, you will be able to get results and support that can put you on a path to building your real estate empire.

Where is the Money?

Banks, Friends, Sellers, Investors are some of the ready sources of funds available for you to borrow money. All of us are very much aware that banks lend a majority of the money used to buy real estate, however, don't discount the other sources of financing. Being open to financing from a variety of sources can be the difference in getting a good deal that could pay you dividends or sitting on the bench waiting for a perfectly structured bank financing deal.

I remember when I bought my first home, I was afraid to get a loan from the bank. I knew it was necessary but I had these thoughts that they wouldn't think I was good enough or maybe my profile wasn't good enough or maybe I couldn't do it. I know this thought is still not uncommon because I talk with women all the time who somehow believe investing or homeownership may not be for them.

To the contrary, what I found when I met with the mortgage broker was that I was a pretty good loan candidate. I had a job, I had good credit, I could afford the payments, and it was a cream puff deal for the loan officer. So I had amassed all this stress and anxiety for myself because none of my 24 year old friends were buying houses. Just because those around you aren't doing it, it doesn't mean that someone isn't doing it and it doesn't mean it isn't for you.

If you've gotten this far in the book, you obviously are interested in beginning an investing career and you're committed to getting the skills necessary to achieve your goals.

Who does it?

Borrowing money to build wealth is something done by the wealthy all the time. They may call it using leverage or investing. The point is that owning real estate and lots of it can give you a lot of leverage to help fund your dreams, finance a business, or invest in other ventures. It all starts with ownership. The smart know that it doesn't take all of your money to own-just the ability to leverage what you have to get what you want.

Why will they do it?

Real estate has long lasting value. And most likely it is going to appreciate over time. If you have any real estate long enough you will see that it is worth more after it builds equity.

Banks know this. Seasoned investors know this. Most average Joes know this too if think critically. Real estate has been the financer for many college educations, many home improvements, many businesses, and more. Because the value is continuing to go up you can not afford to wait to invest.

As a realtor, I work with many first time homebuyers. Some are very young and some are not that young but they've waited to become a homeowner. It amazes me that many people realize they should own a home, that there are positive quality of life benefits, that there are tax benefits but many people don't think beyond these benefits. They don't look at their home as a wealth building vehicle. We missed this point in our education and career building. Unless we've had some exposure to what it takes to build wealth, we may not even think about real estate until later in our lives.

The time is now and banks and investors are out there making loans daily. The question is will we ask or continue to wish. There are many sources available to any property buyer that can take the place of using your own savings account towards the purchase of a property. The following are the top ten sources of a loan that any buyer can tap into:

The Bank
Private Lenders
Investors
The seller
Life Insurance Policies
Assumable Mortgages on the Property
Home Equity Lines of Credit
Lease Options
Partners
Government Programs

1. The Bank, The Mortgage Company, The Lender…

Call them what you want but the first place to start is with the traditional lender. This is the most common finance source and one not to be afraid of or leery of. Don't be afraid—See the Banker anyway.

Many people like to wait until they have all their down payments saved, their credit in good shape, and another tax return before they go and visit a bank. Go anyway. Find out what type of loans are available, what type of programs, how you are viewed by a lender, and what type of money is required. Most good lenders if they don't pre-approve you on the spot will give you a list of things to do to get in "lend able" shape. This is a goal of yours so find out what you need to get the money you need to help achieve your goal. You might be amazed that the lender has a no money down program or you may qualify for a special grant in the area you are buying. Ask lots of questions and you'll be amazed by the answers. I recently met with a new loan company to try to see what types of programs they offered and was amazed with the loan limits I could qualify for and the creative loan packages now available.

2. Private Lenders

I recently was talking with a client who desired to get a mortgage on a property and her credit score was 420. She had already met with a lender who uses private investors and was approved for the loan with a 13.5% interest rate.

Wow! I was in shock. Although FICO scores range from 300-850, I had never worked with anyone with a score that low and she was able to get financing. Now this was a terrible interest rate when the going rate was 6.5% but she was able to get the money she needed.

Some private lenders are also known as hard money lenders. When my husband and I started out owning our own business, we looked at hard money lenders as one possible financing source because of the loose requirements. Before considering a loan that may look like a bad deal from the surface, I would ask that you consider the following questions:

Does the appreciation or the equity in the property outweigh the interest rate I'm paying on the loan?
How long will I keep this loan and this property?
Can I afford the payment?
Does this loan put me closer to my financial goals?
Is this my last resort or are there better financing options?
What benefits would I have with waiting to obtain a loan?

So my point is don't rule yourself out from getting a loan with a terrible credit score or if you don't have a "cream puff" profile. If your score is low, you should work on improving it. However, until you have things turned around it is nice to see with unconventional and private lenders you can still receive the money you need to move towards your goal.

3. Identifying Investors

I remember when I was 16, I really wanted this car that cost $2500. I had been working and had saved close to $1500 but I was still short. My family didn't have any money and I had no idea where to get a loan. My first lesson in life with putting a question on the table was meeting with my best friend's father and asking for a loan. I'll never forget we went to McDonalds and had breakfast and I laid out my case. I told him that I was working, I could pay him X amount per month, and that he could be a huge part of investing in my future. I think he was shocked that I came to him with such a proposal. I also think he cared about my success and my future. And I know he had the money to invest. So, wow, it worked and I paid him back every cent. You may not know who is willing to invest in you unless you ask.

Possible Investors might be any of the following:

Seasoned real estate investor in town-He may be tired of going out there and rehabbing properties or dealing with rentals but may see the value in the process. He or She also may have properties that they want to sell at a reduced price.
Investment Club Participants—See if there is a real estate investment club in your town and go to a meeting. Start one with the women's group at your church or you're civic
Friends and Family-If you don't have the money or the credit, who in your family does? Can you convince them to join you in a business venture? You show them the numbers, you do all the work, they put up the money, and you split the profits.
Fellow Beginner–Maybe you qualify but for only a portion of the loan value you need. Is there anyone else out there that is interested in getting into real estate. Can you collaborate on a deal and split any profits.

Start with the bank but don't be afraid to think beyond the bank. Collaboration may be the answer to help you reach your financial goals.

4. The Seller

Flexible sellers can be one of your best sources for financing of your investment property. Many banks recognize the participation of a seller in the deal as a viable and important source of making a win/win situation for everyone involved in the deal. Approaching a seller with this goal in mind, will help him to achieve his goals and you to achieve yours.

Seller assistance can come in variety of forms. We will discuss them in the following top ten strategies. Sellers can participate in the financing of the mortgage by either entering a land contract agreement or by carrying a second mortgage with your bank or investor mortgage. If the seller agrees to provide financing of the mortgage, you will compose an agreement that will indicate how much the seller is loaning you, how much the payments will be, and the length of the loan. This mortgage is recorded on the property as a second mortgage after the primary mortgage just like you would do if you obtained a home equity or traditional second mortgage.

I have seen sellers who may have so much equity in a property that they are already making money on the first mortgage and are willing to wait on the remainder of the proceeds from the sale if they are given an attractive interest rate or an attractive offer price. It is possible for the seller to benefit more from being flexible than selling the property at a lower price. So don't rule out the seller. Finding out why a seller is selling may give you answers and ammunition to construct a mutually beneficial deal.

5. Borrow Against your Life Insurance Policy

Do you own a whole life policy that you have been paying on for years? Whole life insurance policies are one resource of cash available to you to borrow from without any hassles of verifications or credit scores. Any financial advisors or insurance salesman are cringing at this point because some people will borrow against their policies and not pay the money back. This is an investment in you and your real estate career and your family's financial wealth. Any outstanding loans will be deducted from your death benefits. So make sure you purchase some term insurance in the meantime until you pay yourself back.

I checked my whole life policy and was surprised at the amount of cash value that is starting to grow. This is just another resource that may help you to get started in an empire that will continue to pay you and your family as long as you own the property. So explore your cash value. You originally signed up for the more expensive policy so that you would have the flexibility to use those funds at a later date to invest in yourself.

6. Assumable Mortgages on Property

Assumable mortgages can be a great way to obtain a loan with very little down. Many mortgages issued now are not assumable there can be some benefits of assuming a mortgage for buyers. As interest rates continue to rise in the post Greenspan interest rate era, I think assumable mortgages may gain more appeal.

So how does an assumption work? The buyer takes over the payments or assumes the current mortgage and interest rate that a seller has on his property. The buyer will also take on all the responsibility of the mortgage just as if the loan were given to him originally. The biggest advantages of assuming a mortgage are better terms which typically include a lower interest rate and the absence of as many closing cost fees.

Some points to consider when considering an assumption:
The lender must approve the assumption
The Seller is still held liable for loan if the buyer defaults
Lenders don't look at these loans favorably and may try to adjust the interest rate or charge additional fees
The buyer has to still qualify for the loan with the lender

If you do find a seller with an assumable mortgage, always ask if he is willing to allow you to assume the payments. In different markets, sellers may be more flexible to get rid of the payment. In this case you may be able to create a win/win situation for you both.

7. Home Equity Lines of Credit

If you already own a home or some type of property, you may want to leverage that property to help fund your new property ventures. I have a friend who was willed a very inexpensive home from her grandmother upon her grandmother's death. She didn't think it had very much value but the property was free of debt and liens. As a small business owner, she was having more difficulty getting the type of loan that she wanted for a first mortgage because of income verifications and producing all of the documentation.

When she decided to use this little house her grandmother left her, she found it was easier for her to get a loan because she was actually doing a refinance versus a first purchase. Refinances are usually cheaper, faster, and easier to approve than first mortgage purchases because you show that you already own a property and you already have assets. Property ownership has power!

8. Lease Options

Another seller backed financing choice is the Lease Option. If you don't have money for a down payment or have credit or financing issues, lease options may be a viable option.

Lease options work by you (the buyer) entering into a contract with the seller for a predetermined price and time frame. In the meantime, you as the lessee are able to occupy the property or in some cases sub lease it to another tenant buyer while you are working on obtaining financing. If this period is a year or 2 years you may find that you want to sell your option to someone else. These are a little complicated for your first deal but we will discuss these a little more in Power Play number 4 when we discuss buying with no money down.

9. Partners

Much like investors, partners may be an important asset as you move on this path to financial freedom. Teamwork and combined resources can make securing a loan easier as well as splitting the workload on properties and management. Partnerships like marriage can take strange courses if one partner feels that the other partner is not carrying their own weight or if finances are strained throughout the transaction.

The idea of a partner is great because that means the responsibility and the resources are spread around. Before entering a partnership, evaluate the benefits of partnering with that person. If found that sometimes it's easier to have someone as an investor and have clearly defined roles. This way someone may be a partner financially but will not have any management responsibilities.

Government Programs

Programs exist in abundance to promote homeownership and safe, clean, affordable neighborhoods. Tap into government programs if they exist in your city. These programs are designed to help people own homes and make properties more affordable to purchase. Some programs can provide up to 5% in down payment assistance to first time home buyers. Some will provide funds to help rehabilitate a property to livable and sustainable conditions. I have the most luck finding out about programs from neighborhood housing resource organizations, community lenders, and Department of Housing and Urban Development.

You may also find that your city or state government may also have programs that give handsome gifts to buy in certain zones of the city and may offer forgivable loans. I have seen people buy lots for as low as 1 dollar. Most of the programs may have some stipulations as it relates to time of ownership and owner occupancy so ask a lot of questions.

Many people envision buying a home or investment property as a long arduous task that happens a few times in ones life. This may be the case for some people but there are those of us who are out there everyday involved in a new creative and exciting deal. Don't shy away from the process. Using other people's money and funding sources is a smart way to build wealth. It only takes going through a few deals and it becomes easier and more seamless with each new transaction. I challenge you to see which of these tips will work for you and start building.

The next power play will look at many of these financing strategies and how you can craft no money down deal. Buying with no money down will give you more flexibility, more power, more money, and more wealth.

POWER PLAY #4

Buying with No Money Down

As you buy your first investment property or your 20th, the following concepts will be very important to you as a buyer and seller. Buying with no money down will help you to stretch your money further, build more equity, and more wealth.

Creative financing strategies are not mysteries to many in the industry, however, if you are new to real estate it may seem like it's a foreign idea. Many of us think of deals in the most archaic and traditional forms because that's all we've had exposure to.

Many techniques can be combined, prioritized, or sorted to your pleasure. You will find that some techniques you will prefer. You will also find that your realtor or your seller may not be aware or comfortable with every strategy but as you build up your knowledge and skills, you can help to educate them on simple ways to make a win/win for all involved. I've stuck with my top 10 favorites. These are the same strategies used by the pros but available to anyone.

Top 10 Strategies to Buy with No Money Down
100% Lender Financing
Lender Financing and Seller Second
Assumable mortgages and seller seconds
Lease Option Agreements
Purchase or Buyer Credits
Land Contract Agreements
Government Financing
Using Investors
Equity or Bridge Loans
Built In Funding

Strategy 1. 100% Lender Financing

What:

Financing by lenders has gotten loose throughout the years and many are offering very low to 100% financing on investor loans. If you are a "cream puff" buyer, I would suggest this type of financing as your best option if you don't have a motivated seller who is offering a gravy financing deal. Working through a lender gives a new investor a chance to move through the process with fewer mishaps because you will be working with an established lending institution.

Who:

This loan may only be available to someone who has good to great credit, is in a state where this program exists, and has a solid lending profile. Many new investors may also feel comfortable beginning their investment career within a more traditional system. The approval or disapproval of this type of loan is based solely on you and your profile.

Why are lenders doing this?

Many lenders have seen the need to be creative in providing owner occupant and non-owner occupant investor loans. Search for companies that are offering 100% financing offers. These deals are less available at your big bank but some mortgage brokers or private lenders may offer this financing.

Benefits

The benefits are numerous for this type of deal. Some of the benefits are as follows:
Working with established lending source—Lenders are in the business of lending money. Working with an established lending source will ease any anxiety associated with your purchase.
Lender is familiar with constructing the 100% loan—If the lender is offering this program he is familiar with how to get the loan to close.
Simplified process—It's definitely a more simplified process when you are working with one lending source and do not have to simultaneously pull together multiple funding sources.
Only one payment to one source—One payment will make bookkeeping and profit margins clear and simple.

Very Little Negotiation-With a bank you will apply and get approved. You will most likely not have to talk the bank into the financing structure and negotiate carry backs like you would need to with a seller.

Strategy #2.

Lender Financing with Seller Second

What is this?

Lender financing again is your most simplified way of getting your loan funded. This is the way that most of us will be getting our loans funded. The seller second is a loan that you negotiate with the seller to cover any difference in the main loan and your lack of funds. For example if you are approved for an 80% loan on a $100,000 property, the bank has agree to loan you $80,000. If you have no money and would like to have a 100% Deal, you might try to negotiate a second mortgage with the seller for $20,000. Some sellers have to be offered incentives to agree to this deal such as a high market price offer or an attractive interest rate to carry the loan.

The seller is then acting as a bank and will take second position on the loan title and must be paid off when the property is sold.

Who's involved?

After getting approval by the lender, you will have to find sellers who are motivated enough to carry a second mortgage. Some sellers won't be familiar with this process and may be reluctant to provide this as an option. However, a motivated seller may provide the financing assistance you need to create a win/win situation.

Benefits
The benefit to you the buyer is that you get 100% financing
The benefit to the seller is that he may be getting a higher than normal price for the property
The seller will collect the interest that you owe while he is carrying the loan.
The seller receives a steady stream of income.

Strategy #3
Assumable mortgage and seller second mortgage

Using this strategy you will identify a seller who has an assumable mortgage. Assumable mortgages could be ARM mortgages, FHA mortgages, or other assumable mortgages. By using this strategy you are able to tap into the sellers existing mortgage on the home and assume his current terms and conditions. You then will become responsible for the mortgage and make the payments directly to the bank. The seller second mortgage may be necessary if the seller's payoff is less than the market value of the property.

Assumptions are beneficial because they can give you an opportunity to obtain the mortgage at a lower rate or better terms than you could get on your own. The seller second is beneficial for you because again it allows you to enter the situation with no money out of pocket and without extensive qualifications.

Why would a seller do this?

People always ask me why a seller would be so flexible. You never know what type of situation a seller may be in that would cause them to be flexible. It could be a job transfer, a divorce, a bankruptcy, a vacant home. The seller may have 2 mortgages. The house may have been on the market for a year without any viable offers. Look for these sellers and you will have a great chance to put together a flexible and creative deal that can be a win/win for all involved.

A seller could also do this for the added benefits the seller can receive by selling his home to you with delayed benefits versus selling it for fewer benefits today. Keeping in mind "What's in it for the seller?" will help you craft better offers and find solutions that everyone can live with.

Strategy #4 Lease Option Agreements

Lease options are great tools that when used correctly can help both the buyer and seller achieve their real estate goals. A lease option is a contract that is entered into by the buyer and seller that the seller will give the buyer tenancy in the property, and she also has the legal right to purchase the property on or before a specified time for a particular price. By entering into a lease option with the seller, you agree to lease to own the property and predetermined payments. The seller agrees to sell you the property under certain terms that are already spelled out in a contract. This is an option and you have the choice to exercise it or not.

Many investors love these types of contracts because it gives you control of the property without owning it. Specifically there are several benefits that make this an attractive strategy:

Low or no initial costs to the buyer.
Buyer has possession and control of property.
Buyer has right to walk away if value does not meet expectations.

The seller also has benefits that include:
Price is usually on high scale of market value.
The option may be null and void if the tenant defaults on payments.
The seller receives tax deferred option money.

Strategy #5 Purchase of Buyer Credits

It is possible to reduce the amount of funds brought to closing by collecting purchase credits at the closing. Credits are any funds paid on your behalf at closing. This could be rents that have already been collected, security deposits, closing cost credits, down payment assistance, inspection credits, and repair credits. Whatever you can think of can be added as a credit.

In order to obtain credits at closing, all items must be agreed upon in the offer to purchase. Lenders may also have limits on how much assistance the seller can provide with loan costs or down payment costs. Ask the question because it may be enough to get you a no money down deal or in some cases a check back at closing.

An example of this could be a house that costs $100,000 and requires a 10% down payment. In the offer to purchase you negotiated with the seller that he would pay all closing costs and 3% of the loan in down payment costs. If this is a 2 unit that rents for $600 per unit and the seller is holding $1200 in security deposits, you will get credit for this as well. If you are closing on the 15th of the month you will get half the rent on both units. The seller has also agreed to pay $2500 for new carpet in each unit. So what would this look like?

Purchase Price	$100,000
Loan amount	$90,000
Down Payment	$10,000
Minus purchase credits	
3% of down payment	($3000)
Prorated Rent	($600)
Security Deposits	($1200)

Carpet Credit	($5000)
Water Bill	($200)
Total Credits	$10,000

It's possible. I've seen it. Even if the bank won't allow the seller to participate but so much, there are other things such as repair costs that may be negotiated. Each bank will vary with how strict they are.

Strategy #6
Land Contract Agreements

Another financing source where the seller acts as the lender is the land contract. In land contracts the buyer pays most or all of the money for the property to the seller before receiving legal title to the property. Similar to a lease option the buyer does obtain tenancy of the property but acts as the owner and the seller serves as the lender. If the buyer defaults on any payments, the seller is required to enter into a foreclosure process just like a bank would. Some states differ on their use of contract and some individuals perceive them as nothing more than a lease option.

The major difference is that the buyer is paying down an amount. For example if the land contract is for $50,0000. The buyer would make 100 payment of $500 and then regain legal title of the property. This figure of course does not include interest. Adding in interest would make the payment higher. The contract may also stipulate a shorter time period such as 1 year or 3 years before buyer regains legal title and require a balloon payment. What typically happens is that the buyer is working to get financing during this period to buy the seller out of the agreement.

It is important to remember that this agreement is for passing of title at a future period time. Anything could happen between the time that the buyer actually takes ownership. The contract should spell out exactly what happens in the event of a fire. It should also protect you, the buyer, from the seller undergoing divorce, bankruptcy, death, or mental incompetence.

Some other points to consider:
Have your land contract drawn up by a real estate attorney.
Run Title before you enter into the contract and before taking ownership.
Clearly specify all potential changes and risks

Strategy #7
Government Financing

There are numerous government loans out there that have built in financing that could give you a no money down deal. Government financing could be a great deal because it may have a low variable interest rate or require less stringent qualifying than a typical new mortgage loan.

Where do you find Government Financing?

Government Foreclosures may offer financing and be funded by the local housing authority, city, county or state government housing program.

HUD or VA Houses may have financing available for their properties. In some cases they may also loan repair costs. HUD and VA typically use the same local brokers who have the contracts for their listings.

New Property Financing may be available. In some cities that are revitalizing the community, they may offer financing for new construction homes in the area.

Check HUD, VA, and city or state websites. Sometimes the properties for some programs may not be listed in the MLS. Find out where all the properties that may be sold are listed. Check these listing regularly for great deals.

With all of these government backed financing programs; you want to be sure to check the occupancy and ownership timelines of the property. Some programs may want you to own the property for 5 years or pay a fee because of the discounts you received.

For example, in my city, the state housing commission offered low rates for purchasing homes in a certain community. These rates were about half of market rates. This program also included a grant to cover the down payment of the house. On the surface this seemed like a great deal, however, when I looked into it further, there was a prepayment penalty on the loan. The prepayment penalty would not allow a sale of the property without paying back the ownership incentive.

Each state will vary on its guidelines. Some may not have a prepayment penalty but allow another to assume the mortgage. Whatever the case, know the process before proceeding.

Strategy 8
Using Investors

Maybe it's your uncle or aunt or friend from college. There may be someone out there willing to invest in your real estate pursuits. You will never know unless you ask. As you build your networks and discover people who may have the money or credit and do not have the desire to do the work, you may locate an investor.

Why Investors?
Investors allow you to leverage the money or credit of another and create a win/win for both of you

Will anyone invest in me? If you are a sound business person and have shown you have a history of success, why wouldn't someone invest in you? In order to attract this person or persons, you will also be limiting their risk by giving them an ownership interest either in the property or the deal. You don't need to own everything in order to profit from it. In fact, I read once in real estate you want to own nothing and control everything. The same is true with obtaining investors. If you can show your Aunt Betty how she can double her money for retirement by taking a home equity loan out against her paid off property, would she be interested. You have to show an investor what's in it for them. All they are doing is putting up some money and you are doing everything else. You are putting their money to work for them instead of sitting there doing nothing.

Where do you find investors?
Friends or Family
Affluent people you know
Lawyers or Doctors or other busy professionals
Local investment clubs
Women's Groups

I've found that I you are creative, ask, and always think win/win that you are more compelling when developing a partnership.

Strategy #9
Equity or Bridge Loans

If you own another property and need a down payment on an investment property, you can typically obtain an equity loan or bridge loan very easily against the equity in the property. Some investors like to keep a line of credit against one property or collection of properties because it can work just like cash. A $50,000, $100,000, or $200,000 line of credit might just cover your down payment on a property or cover the cost of the property itself.

The advantage of using an equity loan is that you are not making new paper or new inquiries. You basically are your own bank and you borrow from yourself and pay yourself back as properties are sold.

If you don't have that much equity, that's okay as well. You can use a traditional first mortgage on the new property and leverage the equity in your primary property to create a no money down option for yourself.

It's important that these loans are used only for real property, repairs, or some thing of value. The worse thing that could happen is if the equity in your home is whittled away on useless items. If the bank wants you to cash out, resist unless you have a definite purpose for the money.

Strategy #10
Use Built In Funding Sources

Much like the government foreclosures, there may be other properties out there with built in funding sources. It could be anyone from a small investor group or bank or seller backed funding.

Some examples of Built in Funding Sources are as follow:

1. For Sale By Owner (FSBO) Sellers may offer no money down, assumptions, or seller seconds to entice a buyer to purchase the property.
2. "Financing Available" Ads could be offering financing from private lenders or investors.
3. Seasoned Investors. There are some investors who may have once been in your shoes and realize that new investors always need financing. They may offer financing for a piece of the deal.

The FSBO

As a real estate agent, I've seen it time and time again that FSBO's can eventually get tired, frustrated, and motivated to sell their properties. FSBO's know that if they make financing easy that they could have a buyer. What makes a FSBO motivated?

Despair that there property hasn't sold. They've tried everything and now they are concerned that their property will never sell.
Tired of marketing the property, showing the property and having no buyer. They are ready!
Looking for an honest and decent person to put a deal together. The goal in real estate should always be win/win. A motivated FSBO realizes this.
Do It Yourself/Independent Workers-FSBO's usually fall into this category? Hence they either had a real estate professional and fired them or thought "Hey I can do this." They are likely to also believe that they can handle the financing or work a deal with you.

Financing Available Ads

These ads may have unusual funding sources or private lender sources.
Follow up on these opportunities immediately.
Private Lenders could have less stringent paperwork required
Financing availability may be from non conventional financing source
May have relationship or motivation to finance property.

Seasoned Investors

I recently became aware of a company that caters to investors by setting up a rate of return with a property with a lease option situation and then finding motivated credit challenged buyers to buy the properties. What a great scenario. The buyers basically agree to occupy and care for the property until they can purchase the house themselves and the investor has a guaranteed rate of return because the purchase price is set. Seasoned investors are always looking for opportunities to have their money work for them and if you can show them how they may invest in you.

There are numerous ways you can craft a deal to create a no money down situation for you. Be open to options and opportunities and a deal may be around the corner for you.

POWER PLAY #5

Investing in the Single Family Home

The most common owned, common sold, and most highly desired type of home is the Single Family Home. As a new investor, buying a single family may be the simplest, easiest, and most profitable way to begin your empire. But I want to own large apartment buildings and massive developments, you say. This is certainly possible but I believe it all begins with that first rental home and the first rental should be one that's possible to obtain, possible to manage, and possible to sell.

Don't Get in Over Your Head

The most important aspect of real estate investing is starting. Walking through several properties and sitting down to write an offer on one, shows that you are ready, you have begun, and you are serious about your real estate investment career. I'm encouraging you to start now. Start with the possible in your community. The easiest most possible purchase to make, possible to manage and property to sell is the single family home or single structure.

For me, my first investment was a duplex. I lived in the lower and had a tenant upstairs. If you live in an area that has duplexes this is another great way to begin investing. The best part about buying a duplex that you will live in is that you get all the advantages of an owner occupant as well as the advantages of being a property owner. In many cases, the tenant will even pay a portion or all of your mortgage.

In this chapter, we'll cover what makes a deal. Why starting small and building your way up is the best way for a new investor to get started and how to distinguish a good deal over a bad deal.

Why you don't want a Bad Deal?

Bad real estate deals can cause a lot of pressure and undue stress. I've read many books on finance and met with financial advisors and some have advised against investing in real estate. This intrigued me because I've seen so many people do so well with their real estate investments. Then it dawned on me everyone brags about their good deals and few will tell you how they really messed a deal up.

With real estate, I'm a firm believer there is more good than bad. Because, however, there is a bad I want to address those hang ups and help you to avoid any possibility of a bad deal. All of the horror stories you've ever heard about real estate investors end up the way they do because the investor got in over his head and stopped following basic investor rules:

Basic Investor Blunders

Rushing to buy a property without properly inspecting it
Overpaying for a property because you've not analyzed the market
Buying a Liability instead of an Asset-Property does not cashflow enough to cover mortgage, maintenance and repairs. Property has no equity or property is in a depreciating area
Renting to Bad Tenants that don't pay the rent or destroy your property
Becoming overwhelmed with Property Management and failing to maintain properties
Not following local code compliance or ordinance rules

Why is the Single Family the Way to Go?

Starting with that first single family will help you put into practice the basic investment principals and become familiar with the good and bad of property ownership. The key to ownership is pulling out all the good and then duplicating those exact same results in your other properties.

I read once that you always buy an investment property with the intention to sell. Even if you are not going to sell for years down the road, what is the most commonly sold type of property? If it's single family today. It will most likely be single family tomorrow or ten years from now. At any point in time, there will always be a need for a decent, affordable 3 bedroom single family home. Because of this fact, investing in a single family should always be a sensible and safe investment.

Power Play number four is all about making that first property investment. Finding properties, evaluating properties, and decision making. In this Power Play, we will look at 3 very important aspects of starting your real estate investment career:

What to look for in the area you buy?
What to look for in the property you buy?
Defining a Good Deal.

Researching the Area

Starting with the known is theme of Power Play Number 4. The first known is starting with a known area. This may be the area that you live in or an area that is near. In order to get to know the area even more you should do some research of your area. Some of the things you want to know are as follows:

What are the average values of properties in your area?

You want to be in an area that has moderately priced homes when you are buying for rental purposes. This area may be attractive to first time homebuyers and working class buyers. According to the National Association of Realtors, in 2004, 40% of buyers of homes were first time homebuyers. First time homebuyers will most likely be looking for moderately priced single family homes. If this area is moderately priced and affordable by most today, it should be that way in the future.

What are the trends for the area?

Is this a stable area or are owners making a huge exodus for the area. Even though you may be buying to rent, you don't want to buy in an area that caters only to renters. The danger with buying in areas that may be moving towards a larger rental market vs. owner market is a decline in property value. You want the right now money as well as the future money when you sell the property. Buy with selling in mind.

Look for development trends of shopping areas and new developments. Are shopping areas being built or shutting down. Are vacant lots being developed into new homes or growing into overgrown weeds.

Look for emerging markets

Are there areas that the city has designated as a special zone? Is Habitat for Humanity or other non profits redeveloping an area. Are new condos or shopping centers going up in an area. If you are going to buy and hold, this may be a prime area to get into before the prices begin to escalate to meet demand?

What are the rental rates for the area?

Knowing the rental rates for your targeted areas will help you analyze the feasibility of investing a certain home. I've found the housing assistance program (Section 8) in my area to be very helpful with identifying market rates. The housing assistance program can also be a great resource for finding tenants that have a steady, reliable rental allowance.

Who's attracted to this area?

Understanding who's attracted to this area will help you to understand if you are buying in a suitable investment area. This statement is not designed to break any housing discrimination laws but to analyze the viability of your neighborhood.

Are you buying in an area attractive to a diverse clientele? Will first time home buyers want to live here as well as renters? Will young families as well as senior citizens feel safe in the area? Are there parks, hospitals or schools nearby? How far away is this area from jobs, shopping, transportation?

What to Look for in the Property you buy?

Once you have settled in on an area then you should begin to look for properties that fit within your search criteria. Your search criteria should be set up similar to this:

Decide on what an ideal property would be like.

What is your dream deal? Realistically, this is not going to be a property in perfect condition that is gleaming on the end of the block that requires no sweat and is priced 50% below its market value. However, it is possible to find a property that may need just a little work to make it into a shiny new gem. It is possible to find an extremely motivated seller who's willing to lower his price where you need it. It is possible to run across an overlooked diamond in the ruff.

Most investors want a steal. Hey we all do! I've found it's easier looking for a great deal versus a steal. Many times the steals come back to bite you.

So, realistically, what is an ideal property.

It may be a property that you can acquire with no money down and cashflow $500 a month with at least $10,000 worth of equity.

It may be a property that needs less than $5000 in rehab work and can be flipped to walk away with at $20,000.

It may be a great property that's easily rented in an emerging area that will provide a steady stream of cash flow of at least $1000 a month that needs no work but may require a small down payment.

The ideal property could come in many packages. Deciding the type of packages that you are comfortable with managing will give you a frame of reference for your searches. Always work the numbers and evaluate properties based on your standard or ideal. When you know what you're looking for it will be easier for you to identify it when you find it.

2. Look for homes with Universal Appeal

Buying homes that have universal appeal to most people will make your investment career much more fun and profitable. It is very tempting to purchase those properties that are disguised as good deals in an awkward package. I've been tempted to buy these because I think the cashflow is good or the neighborhood is pretty good. The third key is universal appeal. If the appeal is not there, it's probably a pass.

What's a P.A.S.S.? A Property Attaining Sub-standard Status. This could be the old church that has been turned into a 4 family apartment building and has one apartment that requires entry from another unit. This could be the only house turned sideways on a hill in a neighborhood of similar looking homes on flat land. This could something as simple as the single family that has just 1 bedroom the size of a closet.

We will be tempted by P.A.S.S.'s everytime we go out looking. They will be those properties that have been on the market a while and we wonder why no one has bought it because it seems to be in a decent area or it has a great price on it.

To avoid buying a P.A.S.S., look for homes with Universal Appeal.

Homes with Universal Appeal will have the following:
Nice Sized Bedrooms
A Home with at least 2 Bedrooms, 3 Bedrooms in a Family Friendly Area
Large Kitchen
Bathroom near bedrooms
At least 2 parking spaces or a Garage
Attractive Exterior (Curb Appeal)
Similar looking homes around it (Neighborhood Appeal)
Homes with Showers
Standard Home Features

3. Inspect for potential and worse case scenario

When I'm inspecting a property I evaluate for the potential as well as worse case scenario. This was a hard practice for me to start because I'm usually an optimist who likes to believe in potential and best case scenario. With real estate, I've learned that I must not only look at potential but also the worse case scenario and then I'm likely to make a more sound decision.

For example, if I know a property probably needs a new roof and the home inspector confirms that the roof is at the end of its useful life, then I should plan for the roof needing to be replaced immediately even if it's not currently leaking. Even though a property has great potential, I know I must plan for worse case scenario because I want to ensure my numbers work out in the end where I am still profitable as an investor.

By inspecting for potential I like to ask myself some of the following questions: Where will this neighborhood be in a year or five years? If I replaced the vinyl tile with ceramic tile, what would that do for my value? What could this house look like if it were completely cleaned out with new carpet and with a fresh coat of white paint? Could I live here?

The worse case scenario questions I would ask are as follows: What does that brown spot on the wall mean? What's the most it would cost to rehab this property? How long can I go with out this place being un-rented? What's the least I would get on the market for this place? What would prevent someone from living here or wanting to buy this house?

By keeping it in perspective and looking at potential as well as worse case scenario, I've profited on every deal I've been involved with so far in my career.

4. Seek professional Advice

Most of us are not contractors, builders, or home inspectors so in order to ensure we are making good buys, we should enlist the help of inspectors and contractors. I believe in everyone having the ability to make a living and certainly there are a lot of people within the field of real estate trying to get a piece of the pie. This is an advantage for us as investors because we are able to acquire the knowledge of experts and make our deals faster and more efficiently.

Using inspector and contractors will help you to make more accurate estimates of repairs and help you to more accurately assess the condition of a property. Once you develop relationships with many contractors they will come out for you at no cost and make assessments with the hope of performing the work for you if you buy the property.

5. Look for properties with a Financing Hook

A property with a financing hook can come in a variety of packages. This can be the key to acquiring a good deal. Look for properties with Seller backed financing, no money down program, VA loans, Assumable mortgages, Tenant occupied already.

One property we found with a financing hook. I was purchasing a duplex as an investment property. In researching the property, we saw that the seller was holding two sizable security deposits. Working with the PHH mortgage, we were able to obtain a 7% down financing deal on an investment property and we negotiated with the seller that he would cover 2% of the down payment and closing costs. Additionally, we closed in the middle of the month and were given credits to cover the code compliance repairs. I am a licensed Real Estate Broker so I get paid from my company on any deal that is listed in the MLS. I did have to put down Earnest Money but by the time I got to closing I had so many credits from the security deposit, seller assistance, rental credit from two rented units, and commission income that I actually walked away from the closing with extra money as well as instant cash flow on 2 occupied units.

How does that work?

Purchase Price of Property	$80,000
7% Down	$5600
Earnest Money	($1000)
Closing Costs	$2000
Total Costs	$7600

2% Seller Down Payment Closing Cost Assistance	$1600
Rent 2@550 credit for 15th Closing	$560
Credit of Security Deposits	$1600
2.4% Commission Income	$1920
Code Compliance Credit from Seller	$500
Total Credits	$7600

For us the deal worked out too perfectly to pass on this property. In addition to it having instant cash flow, we weren't out of any money on the front end, and with just a few cosmetic repairs, we knew we had a minimum of $15,000 in equity.

Some of the items, you'll notice are the security deposit credits and commission income. These are items that may have to re appropriated to my trust account however there is no immediate pressure to bring large sums of money to closing.

Price and terms are equal in defining a good deal. I also like to add "pressure" to this. To me an ideal deal is one that doesn't involve a lot of pressure to make it work. I want to work smart and efficiently but I want deals that allow me the flexibility to work on the repairs when they are going to be most feasible and affordable. For example, if a house needs a lot of outside work I don't want to be forced to work on it in dead of Wisconsin winter. I would rather it be cash flowing until the spring or summer when it makes more sense finish the outside repairs. It this property already has a tenant in a lease then I have the ability to do this without it costing me any money to hold on to the property.

Defining a Good Deal

How do you define a good deal?

Value, Cashflow, Equity are three considerations when searching for a good deal. Just like I said to buy with selling in mind, you have to buy with Assets in mind. Some people think that just because they are purchasing a property that they are acquiring an asset. Some people also think just because a property has equity that it is good deal for you.

Having equity is great when it is properly leveraged. It is not a good idea to have tons of equity that cannot be leveraged. How does that work? Well, let's say you buy a property that has $10,000 equity but it requires you to spend $20,000 in repairs to make it saleable. This is not a good deal.

Also some risks are not worth taking. I had an opportunity to purchase a property that experienced was a total loss in a fire (a car that can't be fixed—insurance buys it out). The outside looked great but the inside was totally damaged. We received repair estimates that made $20,000 swings. We knew once it was rehabbed that it could easily sell to a family or first time homebuyer. It was a brick bungalow with 3 bedrooms, dining room, spacious kitchen, bath and ½, nice neighborhood, and much more. So what was the problem.

This would have been my first rehab! The repairs were going to cost way more cash than I had available! I shopped the deal to a few investors and no one was willing to help! We would not be able to get a mortgage because of the extent of the repairs! Because the insurance company had declared the property a total loss, it would need zoning approval to be deemed habitable! If presented with that same deal today, I don't know if I would take the same risk. I have more resources available to me today so it would be doable but it would not be done without a ton of pressure.

In order to evaluate properties properly, I recommend asking yourself the following questions before making an offer:

Will this property give an immediate financial benefit plus long term benefits?
Do the repair cost plus the purchase price provide me with a wholesale cost?
Does the property have favorable price and terms?
Does the property cashflow after all expenses and repairs?
Does this property deplete my cash reserves?
Is this an asset and not a liability?
How much equity am I buying into?
Can I leverage this property for other deals?
Would I be able to sell right away and make a profit?
Does this property provide me with more flexibility or less flexibility?'
Considering the potential and worse case scenario, what are my profits?

By asking yourself those questions and following the investor Basic Rules for Success you should be off to a successful real estate career.

10 Investor Basic Rules

Start your investment career with one unit or the Single Family Home
Always purchase an Asset and not a liability
Buy with the intent to Sell
Buy in attractive and emerging areas

Look for homes with a Universal Appeal
Don't buy more problems or repairs than you can handle
Use the advice of experts
Look for properties with a Financing Hook
Work the Numbers on Every Property
Always buy properties that give you more flexibility vs. less flexibility

POWER PLAY #6

Understanding Foreclosures: The Play by Play

Anyone who owns a home has the potential to be in foreclosure. Foreclosure is not just owners who haven't paid their mortgage and now the bank is taking action. Foreclosure can be a result of a person being sued, a death without heirs, taxes, or the IRS. Hardship hits people for a number of reasons and many times a real estate investor can take an unfortunate situation and turn it into a win/win situation.

Many times onlookers may try to make you feel like your profession is not honorable or that you are preying on the misfortunes of others but I have seen over and over where a person may not have any options and selling their home pre-foreclosure may be the out they need to move on with their life. In this chapter, we will discuss the foreclosure process as well as finding properties before they enter foreclosure.

This chapter will not be a quick fix, get rich with foreclosures sermon but a viable option for you to work with as building your real estate fortune. Foreclosures are a necessary product to consider because the only way you will get rich in this game is by buying properties that are under market value. Foreclosures have a high probability of fitting that criteria, however, it is important to note that after this real estate boom of the Bush presidency, many properties may be maxed and refinanced to the hilt and therefore may not be a bargain. Just because a property is foreclosed on doesn't mean it is a great find or steal.

So what is a foreclosure?

Foreclosure is the process of repossessing a property once the owner is in default of his mortgage loan or the process of recovering a debt that is secured by a deed of trust. The process can vary from state to state and bank to bank depending on the laws in a state. The usual foreclosure process is either judicial foreclosure or non-judicial foreclosure.

Each state determines how the foreclosure process will be handled in that state. The judicial foreclosure process means that the foreclosure process is conducted through the court system and usually involves obtaining a hearing, judgment, and court specified waiting period. The non-judicial foreclosure does not include the court system but uses the process specified in the mortgage document. This process varies from state to state and some states may allow both forms of foreclosure.

Why do you care as an investor?

We've all heard stories of people who've bought a foreclosed property for nearly nothing and then they resold it for a huge profit. This is the story that interests so many of us in real estate investing. Many people believe it is quick fix or easy road to riches.

I have to admit this is what interested me in foreclosures. The reality however is that every foreclosure is not a great deal and that the process takes some hard work, persistence, and knowledge. At the same time, there is no lack of resources out there to help you get that knowledge. The hard work and persistence, however, has to come from you.

Back to the story up above...This is the dream of all investors to find that diamond in the ruff. Because this is the dream of all investors there is competition. This competition drives up the prices of properties and makes it harder to get that huge profit. Knowing exactly how the process works though gives you a competitive advantage because everyone doesn't research the process or take the time to purchase the property in the pre-foreclosure state.

Ethics of Foreclosure Buying

Opportunity abounds for new investors as more and more homes are involved in foreclosure. People have asked me "We'll how can you profit off of someone else's misfortune?" or "Don't you feel bad buying someone's home in foreclosure?" Well my answer is "Of course I feel bad for the people" and "I'm okay with the process because I always seek win/win"

I'm perfectly comfortable with purchasing foreclosed properties and pre-foreclosure properties because I always take the high road and I don't involve myself in any transaction that conflicts with my morals and ethics. I also take pride in the fact that any property we have acquired became a better property after we owned it. This has been great for our tenants, neighbors, and the industry. We try to certainly make a profit on any deal we enter but I don't believe you have to make a profit at the expense of someone else losing. When you look at any deal, situation, or relationship, if it's win/win, then everyone gains.

What do I need to know as an investor?

Understanding how foreclosure works in your market will be key to your success as you begin investing in foreclosures. If you are going to participate in buying foreclosures it is very helpful to know exactly how the process works because ultimately you want to find the owner of the property at the very beginning of the process. In my state (Wisconsin) there is a judicial foreclosure process and we are able to locate on the internet foreclosures in our market on the first day the bank files the judgment information.

In states that allow both types of foreclosure, the document used to secure the mortgage loan usually determines whether judicial or non-judicial fore-closure is used. If a deed of trust is used to secure the loan then a non-judicial foreclosure is used while a mortgage usually results in a judicial foreclosure. Some mortgages, however, gives the lender the ability to sell the property without going through the court system if the buyer defaults.

Judicial Foreclosure

Starting a judicial foreclosure involves the lender filing the necessary court action against the owner in default. This is in the form of a pending lawsuit against the owner. This part of the process is important to know because any public action or court action taken is public record and can be viewed by you down at the courthouse. It may be worth taking a trip down to your clerks office to see how foreclosures work if you can't get a clear picture from your research. I'm spending a lot of time on this and offering suggestions because when I started it was very hard to find the information. It seemed that the people who knew the process, didn't want to share or didn't have time to meet with me and then the rest didn't have a clue.

The steps of a judicial foreclosure are as follows:

The mortgager/lender files a lawsuit with the local court. Usually it's with the county circuit court.
The mortgagee/borrower is served notice that he is being sued for foreclosure and advised of a hearing date.
Initial notices are published.

A foreclosure hearing is held and the judge orders the foreclosure of the property or dismisses the case.

The foreclosure sale is advertised where sheriff sales are advertised.

The property is sold to the winning bidder at the sheriff's sale. If not sold, the property is retained by the lender.

A redemption period is set for the borrower to try to exercise his right to retain the property. This may be 30 days to 6 months depending on the state

If the borrower does not settle the judgment then a sheriff's deed is given to the winning bidder after the redemption period.

In a non-judicial foreclosure, the trustee named in the deed of trust has to file a public notice of default to begin the process. If the owner in default does not pay off the default within a certain time frame, the trustee can schedule a public sale of the property. The process is outlined below:

The trustee files a notice of default lawsuit with the local county court or recorder.

The trustee sale is advertised for a minimum required time period by state law.

The property is sold at the trustee sale to the winning bidder or retained by the trustee if the property is not sold.

The borrower may exercise any rights during the redemption or reinstatement period that could vary.

The winning bidder is given a trustee's deed after the redemption period expires.

The following graph shows which states have judicial foreclosure vs. non-judicial foreclosures or both.

State	Judicial	Non-Judicial	State	Judicial	Non-Judicial
Alabama	•	•	Montana	•	
Alaska		•	Nebraska	•	
Arizona	•		Nevada		•
Arkansas	•		New Hampshire		•
California		•	New Jersey	•	

Left					Right		
Colorado		•			New Mexico	•	
Connecticut	•				New York	•	
Delaware	•				North Carolina		•
Dist. of Col.		•			North Dakota	•	
Florida	•				Ohio	•	
Georgia		•			Oklahoma	•	
Hawaii		•			Oregon		•
Idaho		•			Pennsylvania	•	
Illinois	•				Rhode Island		•
Indiana	•				South Carolina	•	
Iowa	•				South Dakota	•	•
Kansas	•				Tennessee		•
Kentucky	•				Texas		•
Louisiana	•				Utah	•	
Maine		•			Vermont	•	
Maryland	•	•			Virginia		•
Massachusetts		•			Washington	•	•
Michigan	•	•			West Virginia		•
Minnesota		•			Wisconsin	•	

Mississippi   •   Wyoming   •

Missouri   •

Who Forecloses

If you get involved in buying foreclosures there are a couple of different avenues to consider identifying a foreclosure. The first point to consider is who is actually foreclosing. The most typical entities involved in foreclosure are the Lender, HUD or FHA, or VA. There are also Tax Lien foreclosures, IRS, and city government foreclosures. We will focus on Lender, FHA, and VA because these are the most common that you will see. In your local municipality you can employ the same tactics you learn about these foreclosure processes to identify the local process.

Many investors may choose to specialize in a certain arena. I have met investors who strictly buy HUD or VA. Then there are some that will strictly buy at the auction. Some may buy from the lender REO department. You will encounter numerous opportunities to buy these properties. Understanding their specific processes will help you yield bigger returns as an investor.

The Lender

Lender initiated foreclosures usually follow very predictable and regulated processes. Especially in a judicial foreclosure state it is easy to find a property that a lender has started the foreclosure process with. Based on the steps listed above, the lender immediately identifies that the property is in default by filing a lawsuit against the owners. Because lawsuits are public information, this information then becomes available to us. This is also prime time to negotiate directly with the owner of the property because the lender cannot actually repossess the property until after a series of steps and due process that usually protects the owner.

The second part of understanding a foreclosure from the Lender perspective is understanding the REO Department. REO means Real Estate Owned. By the time a property is classified as REO it has gone through the whole foreclosure process and now sits with the lender. In theory, an REO property has been rejected and picked over by numerous investors before it hits the banks inventory and certainly before it is listed and reentered onto the market for sale.

Lenders don't like REOs because it means they are losing money. The lender is usually highly motivated to get rid of this property. They are also very secretive about how many they have and they don't just advertise them to the general public. When getting started with investing it may be easier to participate in buying other type of properties. Once you are more sophisticated you can take on the world of REOs directly from the bank. In your local area, you will get to know several companies and real estate agents that will list REOs in the open MLS system.

Sometimes there can be a period of months and years from the time a property first begins in the foreclosure process until it becomes known as REO. An investor then has plenty of opportunity to identify and purchase a property well before it becomes REO.

FHA

When a borrower gets a government backed loan it is typically an FHA loan. FHA is the mortgage insurance division of the U.S. Department of Housing and Urban Development (HUD). HUD homes become available after a person defaults on an FHA insured loan. HUD does not loan the money to the person but insures the money for a lender. When the borrower defaults on the loan, then HUD takes the property back.

Currently, the FHA program has loan limits that vary depending on the type of property but you can expect to find properties foreclosed by HUD for under $200,000 for a single family and under $330,000 for a 4 family unit. For this fact, most HUD properties are usually considered low priced options to buying foreclosures.

HUD properties are listed on the open market as well. You can usually find HUD listed properties on their website at hud.gov. I've also found it helpful to search the local HUD listing agent's website directly once you find out who they are.

These properties can be a great deal for investors but are usually more easily obtained by buyers who want to be owner occupants. Most HUD properties are only available to owner occupants for a period of time before they are made available for investors to bid. Most HUD homes I've encountered usually need quite a bit of work and may also have city work orders that need attention immediately. Sometimes owner occupants may be scared off if the repairs are too extensive. As an investor, I would also be very cognizant of the amount of repair work that is needed to get the property up to par.

VA

Similar to HUD, VA also forecloses on properties. Currently all VA foreclosures are being handled through Ocwen Bank. You can view their listings at www.ocwen.com.

In order to see these properties, you must use a real estate agent to get an appointment through the listing agent.

With both VA and HUD properties, the property goes to the highest bidder. Well isn't that how it always works? Not necessarily. I've found that with banks sometimes you maybe can offer a quick close or a cash deal or higher earnest money and they may let you get a property at a lower price. The government is like a big machine. The deal that nets the most cash wins. My advice for these is getting in and check it out quickly. If the numbers work out then write an offer. For VA there may be a 10 day waiting period or other goofy rules so get your offer in before there is too much other competition by other investors.

Finding a Pre Foreclosure

Buying a property before it reaches the courthouse steps may be the most profitable way to buy foreclosures. Understanding the foreclosure process in your state is most helpful to help you identify properties before they are sold at the courthouse steps.

This process is also not the easiest and it will probably not and should not be the way you buy your first investment property. Why do I say this? Well, I want you to get started. I want you to understand buying investment properties. I want you to understand what it takes to rehab a property. I want you to understand landlording. I want you to feel comfortable with all the financing options. Buying Pre-Foreclosures is next level in my opinion. There are entire books that can teach you about the Pre-Foreclosure process but I want to address it here briefly.

Throughout the processes outlined above is primetime for finding and acquiring a property in the foreclosure process. The key to buying a pre foreclosure is connecting with the property owner. The following five easy steps will help you to find the property owner who is in foreclosure in a Judicial state.

Five Easy Steps to Finding a Pre-Foreclosure without leaving home

Start with a date or list of dates

In a judicial process, judgments are filed daily. Pick a date either today or a few weeks ago to locate owners who've been filed with foreclosure judgments. Review the judgment and other lien holders against the owners. Check for second mortgage holders and equity holders. Sometimes if numerous debtors are listed for this person, it may not be worth pursuing because they may have title problems but make no assumptions, just keep this fact in mind.

You can check these dates by going down to visit the clerk of courts or hopefully by checking the clerk system via the internet. Every county is not online but more and more are going online. Milwaukee county where I live fortunately for me is online and I can complete this step with just a few clicks on my computer.

Get names and addresses of foreclosed property owners.

Get the property owners information. Also find out co-owners. Sometimes the owner of the property may not live at the address of the property so this is why I would look up that information.

After you've found that out I would try to locate their phone number. Check anywho.com or whitepages.com. You would be surprised how many people are listed right there. I've also had success with typing the name into google.com. Many times the name and address and phone number will pop right up.

3. Check them out.

Once I've found out about an owner, I would check them out. I would do this by cross reference their information to the tax system. Milwaukee's tax and assessment information is also online and easily accessible.

What am I looking for on this system. I want to know if the taxes are paid. What the property is assessed at, If there are any special assessments, the square footage of the property, the last conveyance. The last conveyance tells me how long they owned the property and what they bought the property for. This is not necessarily the foreclosure amount because people may have refinanced. This just gives you a good baseline.

I also cross check the owners to see if they own other properties if they have lawsuits or anything I can find out about the owners. It's a shame but there is a ton of information out there just by logging in.

4. Call them

Call the owners if you have their number and see if they are interested in dealing. I would certainly use a script. This will help you to qualify an owners interests quickly.

One word of caution, many people going through foreclosure are stressed out, embarrassed and unhappy about being in this process. They may not call you back or be too interested in speaking with you. So your approach is very important if you do get a property owner to answer the phone.

They may think that you are trying to take advantage of them and will be leery of you. Your goal is to try to create a win/win situation.

5. Get More information

If you get an owner who will talk to you, your goal is to collect information.

Find out what their plans are for the house. Find out what they owe. Find out what type of loan they have (for example is it assumable) Many properties that begin in foreclosure end up being dismissed before the auction because the owners refinance, get a loan, borrow the money, or somehow figure out how to save their home. You do not want to be wasting too much time if the owners have already made special arrangements to save the property.

If they don't know what they are going to do, this is the time to offer solutions. Schedule a meeting with the owners to try to take a look at the inside of the house.

This may seem like a lot of work and it is. Buying foreclosures is a process and one that can be risky but also very rewarding.

The Sheriffs Auction

Bidding for foreclosures on the courthouse steps is a process that can be exhilarating for many investors but also costly and tricky. Before you take your hard earned money down to the auction, I'd like to offer a few tips and realities.

The auction is hard for beginners and I found this out the hard way. The down payments, the old timers, the prices, and the competition are a few of the reasons the auction is challenging to break when starting out. It may be easier for a beginner to buy a house pre-auction than actually at the auction. But by no means, don't rule it out completely, After you've begun your new real estate investment career, certainly check out the auction and learn to play to win.

The following are 10 Real Life Realities of the Auction that makes it challenging for many of us just starting out:

You Do Have to Pay to Play

Bidding at the auction requires an immediate payment or down payment on a property. This down payment is usually around 10% and once you win the bid the funds must be remitted on the spot in cash or a cashier's check. This is great if you've go a lot of cash around but if you're a beginner with very little cash, you won't be able to make it.

You Can't Change your mind

Once the gavel is down and you've forked over your 10% down, you can't go back and change your mind if you find out the property is not worth that much money or you don't want to go through with the transaction. If you do change your mind, you risk losing your 10%.

The Title May Be Tricky

This is a foreclosure you are buying. Chances are if someone hasn't paid their mortgage they haven't paid other bills as well. You wan to make sure this person does not somehow have judgments or liens that may somehow be on the title of the property. If this is the case, then you as the owner are liable for those debts before you can get clear title. You can usually have a title company do a pre-title letter report before you buy but this may be $50-$75 and there is no guarantee you get the property. One good thing to note is that if the debts were obtained after the property was purchased then those debts cannot be added to title.

Competition is fierce

If you find a property that is a great deal, chances are the other investors in the room also have found this property to be a great deal. Because there is a waiting period between the time a property is advertised for sale at the auction and the actual auction, there is plenty of time to research the property and values.

The payoff of the property may start low but after the bidding competition it might just be driven up to market price and then your equity margin may be very low.

Lazy Veterans can sit in the corner and out bid you just so you don't get the property.

This is one of the worst parts of the auction. I call them lazy veterans that sit in the room and will out bid you just so you don't get the deal. How do they do this? Well most of us beginners don't have much cash so if a veteran gets us in a bidding frenzy, he can do one of two things. He can drive up the price of the property so you buy it and spend all your money so you're out of the rest of the auction. Or two, he can chime in and out bid you just because he can to not allow you to get a good deal.

There will be guys in the room with tons of cash who can take lower margins.

Buying Sight Unseen

Sometimes auction properties may be vacant or boarded up or occupied and unavailable to see. Because of this, auction buyers have to buy properties sight unseen many times. You do not want to buy your first few deals sight unseen because who knows what's inside. You want to be able to know and control your expenses when you are just getting started and buying sight unseen can be a risk not worth taking.

You may not be able to finance it

The chance of financing your auction purchase is lowered because of the time limits involved in the sale and the possibility of sight unseen. This is not impossible if you have a good lender who will work with you. I would only recommend financing if you know you can get an appraiser inside the property and you are fully pre-approved by your lender.

Strict Time Limits

Time is of the essence is a reality when buying a property via the government. If they say the money is due in 10 days, they probably mean 10 days, Not 11 days or 12 days or when your loan is approved. Whatever the time limit is to get your cash is usually enforced. Unless you know you've got the money, you want to be careful, because you could forfeit your deposit if you can't get the money by the time limit.

Price may not be worth it

After bidding the price up, I've seen foreclosures that started off as good deals become very bad deals. Just because it's at the auction does not mean it's a deal. Sometimes after a property goes back to the bank, it may become a better deal later because the bank waives some of its fees just to get rid of the property.

Redemption Period of Owners

Most states give the owners a period of time to redeem the property. This may be from 3 months to a year. This is a huge downside to an investor. Imagine you've found the perfect property at the best deal. You went to the auction and placed $20,000 of your limited liquid cash to reserve the property and waited 3-6 months through the redemption period to take possession of the property. Then on the day of the confirmation of sale, the owner shows up at the hearing with a check from a new lender and requests to take back the property. By law you are not able to take possession of the property and the property is returned to the original owner. Your down payment is returned if the owners redeem the property, however, your cash is tied up until this period expires. This is not ideal because if you have limited cash, you want it to be used in a way that it's going to be constantly making you more money.

Overall, buying foreclosures can be a very profitable way to build your real estate empire. These profits will not be made without risk and without caution. Being knowledgeable of all the pitfalls will make this a smoother and more rewarding experience for you as an investor.

In Power Play number 7, we will look at the right way to renovate. We will look at "flipping" and how a girl can play in this male dominated arena. This was my most intimidating road bump on my path to mastering real estate investment. It is necessary and and quite fun to overcome the perception of rehabbing and flipping. If you read no other chapter in the book, this power play will infuse you with the power and knowledge to rehab your way to riches.

POWER PLAY #7

Rehabbing for Riches

Old world charm, hardwood floors, and built in china cabinets attracted me to the very first home I purchased at 25 years old. I loved most of all that the house seemed to be low maintenance with several new amenities, even though, the house was 65 years old. When I first walked in and observed the wrought iron winding staircase, I knew it had to be mine. I had already made my decision prior to entering the bathroom which made me do a double take. The contractors had fully rehabbed the home except for the bathroom. It was absolutely disgusting and I doubted my ability to live with the house with this eye sore of a bathroom. I pressed forward and bought the house anyway, knowing the bathroom would require a complete remodel.

Since I was only 25, single, and wasn't getting any financial support from my family, I had no idea how I would afford the renovations but I stepped out on faith. If I had only known then what I know now or had a mentor to advise me I may have taken different steps but I am thankful for the spirit to persevere. I visited my local hardware store, asked lots of questions, called a few contractors to get bids, and set out to make my bathroom one that was functional, livable, and modern. I received bids from $25,000 down to $5000. All bids were still too high. I could only afford to spend about $2500 on the project. The guys at the do it your self home store helped me believe that I could do it and I took a class on laying tile.

I didn't end up laying the tile myself but I understood the simplicity and steps involved in the process and this was very helpful in my negotiations with the contractor I ended up hiring. Remodeling my little bathroom to the level that I could appreciate and enjoy by myself was one of the biggest confidence boosters I could have had to lead me to move on to bigger and more complex projects. I learned that asking questions are free, many contractors will give a free bid if they think you might hire them, it's up to me to hire whoever I want, and many projects are not as hard as they seem if you have the time and tenacity to make it happen.

This Power Play is written so that a 25 year old single girl who wants to renovate an investment property can find success but also contains tips and tricks I've acquired along the way that may help a seasoned investor ask better questions and price out jobs correctly.

Flipping Properties

In the real estate investment world, the term "flipping properties" can have 2 meanings. The first type of "Flipping" is when an investor has the rights to purchase a property at one price (usually a price lower than market value) does not actually purchase the property but he "flips" it to either another buyer or investor for a profit. For example, if I know of someone who is trying to get rid of a home valued at $120,000 for only $75,000. Maybe they are in foreclosure, there is a death, or a divorce, and they need to get rid of the property right away. I might agree to purchase the property from them for $75,000 and put a contract of sale on the property or an offer to purchase. Once this property is in a contract, I am legally able to purchase this property. I have the ability to assign my right to purchase this property to another person. If I did this and assigned the rights to purchase the property to another buyer at say $95,000. At closing, I would not take possession of the property. The buyer I assigned the property to would take possession of the property. The buyer would then owe me $20,000 because that is the difference in price from $95,000 to $75,000.

Much of the negative perceptions of flipping real estate came from either this practice or the practice of reselling a property right away for a higher price without ever making improvements to the property or determining the true value of the property. Many appraisers and investors have been scrutinized and penalized for this practice when done illegally.

There is no law that says, however, that you cannot re-sell a property in a certain time period at a certain price if both the buyer and seller agree upon a price. Much of the confusion and trouble occurs when banks, government agencies such as HUD or FHA is involved in the deal.

I do not advise anyone to get involved with this type of flipping right away unless you have fully investigated your local laws and understand exactly what it is that you are doing.

The ReHab/Flip

Many investors will also use the term "flipping" when they buy a dilapidated property, rehab it, and sell it for a profit. In fact, much of the general perception considers this practice as flipping as well. I don't like to refer to this practice as flipping because the work is a lot more extensive than just turning a profit in a short period of time. For our purposes we will refer to this as Rehabbing.

If you look at the average homeowner in America, he is constantly remodeling or renovating or upgrading his home. If you live in a house that is 20-40 years old, things are going to break and need to be replaced. Windows are being upgraded, furnaces will run out, paint will begin to chip, the roof will wear out. Then some homeowners may upgrade to get some of the latest gadgets or add on rooms or finish basements. There is always some work to do to a home.

When you look at homes that are abandoned or in foreclosure, they typically will be in need of a lot of this work in order to bring it up to normal standards. This is how rehabbing gets started. Investors may acquire a property at a lower than market price and spend the time and money to improve the property by performing all of the delayed maintenance and bringing it up to a suitable, livable, and marketable standard. I don't view this as flipping at all because there is usually a lot of work that should or could be done to improve the value and the this can be proven to any bank, appraiser, or assessor.

"Rehab able"

Finding a property that is "rehab able" for a profit is your number 1 goal when investing in real estate for a short term profit. Profit is a key word in this sentence. It's not enough to break even and you definitely should not lose money in a rehab. This is where many investors "lose their shirt" or make a lot of mistakes in the real estate market. It is possible to make not only make profits but to make huge profits if you master the 8 Simple Rules for Rehabbing and avoid 8 of the costliest mistakes.

8 Simple Rules to Rehabbing to avoid 8 of the costliest Mistakes

1. Don't Over Pay for the Property-I cannot stress Rule number one enough. You cannot overpay if you plan to unload a property quickly. If you plan to hold onto a property a while in an area that is appreciating at a rapid pace then it makes a little sense. The general rule is never pay more for a property than it is worth—today. Even if it has potential, what is its value as is. You never know what will happen and things always do. You do not want a property that is worth less than the market value at any point. This could be your most costly and devastating mistake of your investing career and ruin hopes for profitability.

2. Price the Job out Right-Not only is it important to pay the right price for a property but you also have to price the work out properly. Sometimes there is an advantage to not knowing because then you call in people who know. If you don't know how much it costs to remodel a bathroom. Call a bathroom remodel or. He'll tell you. He will also tell you why because he will need to justify his prices. Get estimates, get opinions and figure out what you've got yourself into. Almost anything can be repaired, remodeled, or refreshed with enough time and money. You need to know before you do anything how much time and money will be required.

3. Fully inspect the property before you purchase. Unless you are a fully skilled contractor who can handle any job, you need to make sure you inspect the property first. Sometimes in foreclosures or auction sales, it may not be possible to view the property before you buy. I would make sure you have some experience first before you buy properties sight unseen. There may be exceptions but as a rule-Inspect the property prior to purchase.

4. Budget Your Time and Money—What's more valuable than money in real estate? Time! It's important to make sure you accurately budget your time on your projects because the more time you spend on one deal, the less time you have to spend on future deals. Many investors are great with deciding how much it may cost to complete a job but lack an accurate time estimate. If you are purchasing properties on credit or using loans, remember the longer the project remains undone, the more bills you will be paying on the property. Make sure you budget accordingly.

5. Know When to Fold 'Em-Know when to cut your losses if you do make some mistakes. Look at the big picture at all times when completing your rehab. If you are struggling with getting a project completed by your day workers, you may have to spend more money to hire a professional contractor in order to complete the job on time. If a contractor is taking a simple job and making it complex, monitor the situation to know when it starts costing you more money than the task is worth.

6. When in doubt, Just Clean it out-You'd be amazed at how much value is gained just from a cleaned out, fresh smelling, and freshly painted property is worth. We get very muddled in the technical improvements that need to be made. The electrical upgrades, the ailing furnace, the outdated plumbing…I've seen major improvements in a property just by pulling the weeds, cleaning out clutter, and a fresh coat of paint. People buy properties because of an emotional

connection in many cases. They decide up front if they like a property and then calculate the needed repairs.

7. Be Quick but not in a hurry-We've heard this before. Be quick. Move swiftly but don't rush and make foolish mistakes. Foolish mistakes can be very costly.

8. Fix it Right the First Time—Do it right, Fix it right and you'll save yourself lots of hassle and issues. If you try to band aid a job, you'll temporary relief. If you have the electrician there you might as well have him prepare the job properly. The worst thing that could happen if you pay someone to do a lot of work and they don't pull the correct permits or they don't complete the job up to code. If this happens, after the buyer has their inspection, guess what? The work is going to have to be redone.

Contractors

Hiring a contractor can be a scary process especially if you don't have much experience with a particular repair issue. In fact, most of us assume that if we look up contractor in the phone book and ask him to come over to our house to give us a bid, we think that he has to be skilled and qualified because he has an ad in the phone book. Sometimes we also assume that the price that is being charged to us is the general cost for doing a particular repair.

Unfortunately, this is not always the case. My intent is not to bash contractors at all because I believe everyone should have a right to earn a living. However, I do want to alert you to shop around until you find people you trust. There are all sorts of variables and issues that could cause the remodeling of my bathroom to range from $2500 to $20,000. Everything from materials, years of experience, use of licensed subcontractors or workers, use of union workers, professional association memberships, and more.

My goal was to have my bathroom remodeled in an acceptable and affordable fashion for my 1930's first time home buyer house. I didn't want a bathroom that would be featured on Cribs. Many contractors may have a totally different view than what you have on what's acceptable and that's where questions, examples, and knowledge come into play. With your local hardware store available, you can price out materials yourself. They are very helpful with helping to decide also how much a job may cost. Some even have connections with contractors and can make referrals. Prices can vary on labor and time it takes to perform the job, so that's why it's very important to get bids and become good at pricing out a job yourself.

So where do you find a contractor. The easiest way is to ask for referrals. When I got started my pastor at my church gave me referrals, I got referrals from my realtor, and referrals from my neighbor. If you find one contractor that you like, he can also refer you to other contractors that may specialize in different work. Many of these guys may work in an unofficial consortium and refer business back and forth. This could be very good or very bad. One consortium of workers could be thousands of dollars higher than the next. Price is not the only factor to consider when looking for a contractor. You also want to consider quality of workmanship and whether he is bonded and insured. It is important to make sure he's insured because you don't want him to damage your home and you have no recourse.

The F.R.A.N.K Factor

Affectionately named for one of my favorite contractors, Frank, I've developed a simple way to evaluate your contractor by looking for the F.R.A.N.K. Factor in your contractor. F is for Flexible, R is for Reliable, A is for Agreeable, N is for Negotiable, and K is for Keep able.

Flexible-I prefer a contractor who is flexible for several reasons. I want someone is flexible in their expertise. For hard jobs I certainly want a specialist but for rehabbing a house there are usually several issues that need to be addressed. Look for contractors who can help you with many problems unless you just have 1 big problem. Also, look for a contractor who is flexible with your time and with his schedule. If time is of the essence, you will need a contractor who will work with your time schedule to complete your goal. Flexibility is a very important quality to look for in a contractor.

Reliable-Have you ever heard the horror story of a contractor coming a putting a hole in someone's wall and then you not hearing from them for days? Well, reliability is a key quality in looking for a contractor. Sometime I end up with guys who may have multiple jobs and may want to also work on their other projects while managing mine. This is fine if you have an agreement. Never pay more than half up front. If you can pay most of it when the job is complete, that's even better. I like to pay them something up front to get started because it shows my good faith and ties them to the job.

Agreeable-It's always nice to work with someone who realizes that the work needs to be done to your standards and has a positive disposition about completing the work. I look for contractors who are talented, reasonable, and agreeable. This will make everyone who's working on your house work better together.

Negotiable-Everything's negotiable, especially, in real estate rehabbing. Look for contractors who will work within your budget. If a contractor is unwilling to work with you, just move on. Someone will work with you.

Keep able-Use contractors that you will want to use again and refer to your friends and family. Loyalty is very important to small business owners and it just makes good sense. The loyalty that you develop can lead you to deals as well as help you negotiate better deals for the future.

Profits, trust, and a spirit or win/win are the key advantages of looking for contractors with the F.R.A.N.K. Factor. I've found that most people in life just want to make a living for themselves and their family and they want to do it honestly and with integrity. Find the contractors who would like to join your team. They are critical to your success as a real estate investor.

Managing the Contractor

Once you've found a contractor that you can work with, you have to manage the work process. In many climates, contracting is a seasonal job especially if the work involves siding, roof work, or outside painting. Any work on investment houses should be planned out accordingly. April kicks off the busiest season for many contractors and typically prices may increase as well. As an investor, you want to keep this in mind as you budget time and resources on a project. This can work to your advantage if you can get a contractor in a "hungry" part of the season.

You also want to manage the contractor to assure that he stays within budget and within the time goals. Making sure your contractors are on schedule and budget can be one of the most important skills that you will develop as an investor.

Quick Fixes When the Money is Tight

In times when money is not as readily available as contractors, a handyman may be a sensible solution. Listed below are the 30 easiest and cheapest repairs that you and your handyman can complete
Complete clean out
Paint

Light Bulbs Everywhere
Decorating
New Blinds
New Heater Grates
New Outlet and Switch Covers
New Light Fixtures
Updated Thermostat
Wall Repairs
Painted Closet Doors
New Door Knobs
Painted Front Door
New Screen Door
Repair torn screens
Lawn Care and Flowers
New Garage Door Opener
Organized Garage
Freshen Bathroom (Calk, clean, new toilet cover)
Bleach Tile Grout
Clean Gutters
Sweep Sidewalks
Clear, Organized Basement
Wash Basement Floor with water and bleach
Plug Ins
Furnace Filter (vacuum, wipe down)
Batteries for smoke detectors
Tighten Banisters and Railings
Paint Kitchen Cabinets
Replace Cabinet Hinges

Once It's Rehabbed Now What

Once the property is rehabbed you need to reevaluate the market value. Hopefully, before you started with the job you had an idea of what it would take to bring the property up to market standards. Also, you should have had a good idea of what the property values around the property were worth. This is the information that is found either in a home appraisal or a real estate market analysis. Once the property is finished I would perform another market analysis. You're realtor can do this for you, usually for free. The reason I would do this versus an appraisal is cost. Many investors may obtain an appraisal. Unless you are refinancing or have a need for the appraisal, I would settle with the market analysis until the time that you need an appraisal.

Selling your rehabbed unit can be a tense time. You want to make sure that the property is priced accordingly as well as that your costs will be recovered. We discussed working with Realtors earlier. Your realtor will be able to share with you all the costs of selling your home. If the property does not sell right away, find out why. Some of the reasons that properties don't sell are: price, location, condition, market. Find out what is lacking in your property and fix those things. I strongly recommend not listing the property until it is ready to show and sell. The most likely people to buy your home are the first ones who come through and see it. The reason is that many buyers are currently in the market waiting for new homes to pop up. Once those new homes appear they have already seen the competition and they are more motivated to make a decision.

POWER PLAY #8

"Playing for Keeps" Rental Properties as Long Term Investments

Buying and flipping or rehabbing properties is an excellent way to make money and to infuse cash into your business but this is a strenuous process that leaves few millionaires at the end of the day. All the millionaire investors, I've met or read about gained their biggest returns by buying and holding onto properties. In fact, people who bought real estate properties 10 years ago in many cities saw their investments double in under 10 years. Wouldn't we all wish that we bought 1 million dollars in properties 10 years ago. To me this is certainly get rich quick because I know I've been out here for more than 10 years trying to figure it out.

We've all met those people who bought a great house years ago and have seen the value double, triple, or quadruple over time. The key is buying right, staying the course, and having tenants for a long period of time. Enlisting this strategy you are destined for success and riches.

The best part of finding a great deal on a good house is that when you rent it, the tenants pay the mortgage and pay down your debt. The cash flow on this property can also provide you with residual income to build wealth for you over a period of time. There are also numerous deductions and depreciation that you may qualify for when filing your taxes.

But I don't want to be a landlord, you lament. There is definitely a stigma and responsibility associated with being a landlord. This power play is designed to give you some helpful hints for being a successful landlord, how you can set up support systems and processes to alleviate some of the stress of being a landlord, and how to identify and attract good tenants.

When I first considered my first rental property, I shied away and declined the opportunity to own an investment property. I had visions of a tenant destroying my home, appliances breaking in the middle of the night, and all of my money going down the drain. What I didn't have at the time was the confidence and the belief in myself to get the information I needed, acquire the appropriate professional team, and make it happen. Because of this decision, I am further away from wealth at this point in my life. Thank God, I was presented with another investment opportunity a couple of years later and this time my eyes were open to the possibilities.

Being a landlord takes tough skin and professionalism. The following are some of the skills that are necessary for success as a Landlord:

Attract and keep responsible tenants
Consistent, tough but fair, rent collection system
Written rules and regulations
Communication with tenants about expectations
Clean, well maintained properties
Ability to resolve tenant issues promptly
Treating property ownership as a business
Evict irresponsible tenants

Landlording is a business and could be an important stream of income for you and your livelihood. Treat tenants with professionalism and respect but also realize that you have entered into a business arrangement and it is the tenant's responsibility to honor their part of the agreement.

How to attract Good Tenants

Some landlords feel that tenants will take substandard facilities and have little concern for where they live and how they live. The tenants you want to attract do not fall into this breed of folks. The ones that do are not worth your time. I have found that good tenants desire the same things that most homeowners desire. They could be young college students to families to retired seniors. Whoever they are you want someone who pays the rent on time, takes care of your property, and doesn't call and complain all the time. As far as the tenant they want a safe, quiet neighborhood that they can be proud to call home. They want to live in a clean and decent home and want to be comfortable. So where are these people. They are out there and the key is asking lots of questions.

Finding Good Tenants

The search for a tenant is not as difficult as you'd think. It's very easy, in fact, to find someone to live in your property. The key is to qualify this person as someone that would be a responsible tenant. To get the phone ringing, there are simple and cost effective strategies that include using signs, advertising in the classified ads or rental guides, contacting the rental assistance office in your city, or asking for referrals. If you work with property management companies, they may use other techniques and referral services that are more expensive. Most beginning investors can find the appropriate number of tenants using the methods listed above but you may have to explore other options as your holdings grow.

Signage is the first way to attract tenants. It's as cheap as going to the local hardware store and purchasing a sign and sticking it in the window or front yard. This will generate calls from prospective tenants already familiar with the neighborhood or who drive past the property.

Classified Ads are my preferred form of advertising for my market because the ad reaches potential tenants from other parts of the city who may not happen to ride down my street. Also, classified ads are usually viewed by more motivated renters. A sign may generate calls from people just interested in knowing the rental prices in the area. In some situations, you may not want to advertise that a property is vacant if you can't monitor it for vandalism.

Another effective listing is the rental assistance office in your area. If you decide to accept Section 8 or Rental Assistance, the office will typically advertise your unit for free to tenants in need of housing. This is a way to target a tenant that may have a guaranteed payment source.

Using any of these methods are sure ways to get the phone ringing. In your advertisements, it is imperative that you do not break any fair housing laws and provide a favorable description of the property.

The Sorting Process

I remember my very first tenant. She was just okay. She always paid her rent on time but she was not very clean and she had a little boy that was a destroyer. I remember hearing and seeing clues of this when she viewed the property; however, I let her move in anyway. For three years I dealt with her complaining, her little boy breaking items in my house, and the filth whenever we stopped in to do repairs. There were several things wrong with me. First of all, I did not put my foot down. I was pretty good about having her pay on time but there is more involved with a good tenant than paying on time. Equally as important is taking care of your property. People who refuse to replace a burned out light bulb or beeping smoke detector battery are not the type of tenants you want in your house. Questions will help you sort through the type of tenant you desire.

Now I've learned to ask lots of questions. Not discriminating questions but just questions about their lifestyle, their work hours, their babysitting arrangements, their thoughts on being a renter, their expectations, why they are moving, their boyfriends or girlfriends, their smoking and drinking habits. I try to get a clear picture of who is going to be living in my property and how they will take care of it. Since I've started asking more questions, I've been able to get better tenants.

Some other questions you will want to ask are as follow:
1. Where did you live previously and for how long?
2. Who are your previous 2-3 landlords? Get names, addresses and phone if possible.
3. What's your financial background? Get checking or savings account information.
4. Do you have a criminal record?
5. Where do you work? Get names of supervisors or managers.

Many of these questions can be found on the standard rental application that is available at your local legal blanks store. Also you can download a free sample rental application at www.realestatepowerplays.com.

There are now many agencies available to landlords to screen tenants. Some of the services they offer are background checks, credit checks, and reference checks. Whatever process you decide to use just make sure it is comprehensive and effective. You don't need to know every mistake the tenant has made in their life but you do need to know what type of person is going to be living in your house.

So What Determines A Good Tenant?

So what are you looking for and what determines a good tenant. There will be signs right away that will give you an idea if this is someone you'd like living in your property. Has the person lived in numerous places in the last 2 years? If there has been house hopping over the past few years you can probably assume that this person is not the most stable. Either they are moving because they are in financial trouble or they are unable to maintain a long term stable housing. These may be common reasons but there may also be a reason like the tenant can't control such as the landlords keep selling the properties. Whatever the reason it is worth asking the question so you know.

Another indicator of stability is the tenant work history. If the tenant cannot keep a job for more than 3 months then you know there will be breaks in their ability to pay their rent on time. Work history tells you if a person is responsible, if they can get along with others, if they have the ability to pay, and gives you a glimpse of their financial picture. Self employed people are a little bit harder to predict because you cannot verify past performance. Here again is where questions are so important because they will help you get a financial outlook of the person you are dealing with.

I also get recommendations from their previous landlords. This alone will tell a story. Especially if the potential tenant begins to make excuses and complaints about the landlord before you even call. Fortunately for us we have never been sued but I know other landlords who have been reported to the city neighborhood services department or sued because of disgruntled tenants. Some tenants will attempt to have you caught up in mediation or inspections because they know how to manipulate the system. Understanding who you are dealing with is critical to have a win/win business relationship with your tenant.

In my city, the department of neighborhood services offers landlord training. This is a worthwhile course if one is offered in your city. They go over all the laws, ordinances, and rules regarding landlords and tenants. They also connect you with services that provide tenant screening, background and credit checks, and property managers. Knowing landlords is also helpful to understanding certain laws, requirements, or inspections that may be required of rental units.

Keeping Tenants and Good Customer Service

Riding around in many cities, there is a host of For Rent signs. For every vacant unit, is money that is not being made. I was lucky in the beginning of my investment career because I bought a property that already had decent tenants in it and they stayed for a period until the end of their lease. This type of experience can often trick new investors that rental income is all gravy income. Usually, the income does not come without some work and some customer service.

The work involved with keeping a tenant involves the physical work to the property to get it in move in condition, the maintenance of the property, and the communication channels that you establish. All this should be agreed upon up front and maintained throughout the course of the business relationship.

This business relationship leads to the issue of customer service. I have met many landlords who talk down to tenants and believe that they may not deserve excellent customer service. Yes, they may live in your property but they are doing it with the agreement that they pay X amount of dollars per month. Whatever, agreement that you have with them is a two way agreement. The landlord's responsibility is equal to that of the tenant. Customer service must be relayed if you get a letter, maintenance request, phone call, or other question. Treating tenants as you would any customer in another service business is necessary and expected. It takes 1/5 th of the money it takes to retain a customer than to go out and find a new one.

Sometimes making a concession of a few dollars to appease a tenant may be more beneficial than having an empty unit for 3 months while you pay the mortgage and utilities. Keeping communication in the forefront will assure you have a successful landlord/tenant relationship.

Lease Agreements

After you have located a great potential tenant, you want to assure the business arrangement is a success with a written lease agreement. This agreement will list your obligations and expectations as well as the tenants. This will also be your legal enforcing document if you ever need to use it.

There are typically two types of leases, month to month, and fixed-term lease agreements. The difference in the two is the block of lease time that has been agreed upon. In a month to month, the agreement is from one month to the next and renews automatically each month. A lease may stipulate a period of time such as a 6 month lease, 12 month lease, or 18 month lease. It is hard to recommend what type of agreement that you should enter into. This will be based on your needs, the tenant's needs, the type of housing you have, etc. Some leases may be more standard in one area or another. Usually, the lease gives the tenant and landlord a guarantee for a period of time.

Most states may have a standard lease agreement that you can purchase at the legal documents store or office store. It may be a fill in the blank version. A sample lease can be downloaded for free at www.realestatepowerplays.com.

Because state laws may vary on the specifics of the lease, listed below are just a few areas that may cause the average landlord some stress if not addressed appropriately in the lease agreement.

Terms of Lease—Whether it's month to month or 2 years, this should be specified. There should also be a provision for ending the agreement. Is it a 30 day notice, 60 day notice, etc. Having this clearly defined in the lease will alleviate future issues with any tenant.

Rent Due Dates—Clearly defined in this section, should be the agreement for paying rent, due dates, late payments, who to make the check payable to, forms of payments, etc.

Security Deposits-Address the amount of the deposit, state laws for return, and what is required to get this deposit back.

Limits of Use—This section helps you determine who may live in the property and how the property may be used. Watch out for individuals that give you one occupancy number and then another family moves in addition to those listed on the agreement.

Rules and Penalties—This may also be an addendum. This area is where you address appropriate behavior and the right to quiet enjoyment. You may have to enforce these rules if a tenant gets out of hand.

Inspection-This is also an important section, especially tenants. Tenants want the right to live in their property without disruption. This provision addresses what type of notice that will be given prior to entry into the unit.

There are many other provisions that will be included in the rental agreement and other provisions that you may want to discuss such as pets or smoking, etc. It is strongly recommended that you obtain the state laws for rental properties prior to you renting out a property. These laws can be found by searching the web or contacting the Fair Housing office in your town. They will have information on tenant rights, landlord procedures, and possibly a handbook. If you choose to work with a property manager, they should also have this information in their office.

Working with Property Managers

You may want to employ a property manager to help manage your properties. Generally, property and real estate managers handle the financial operations of the property, ensuring that rent is collected and that mortgages, taxes, insurance premiums, payroll, and maintenance bills are paid on time. In community associations, although homeowners pay no rent and pay their own real estate taxes and mortgages, community association managers must collect association dues. Some property managers, called asset property managers, supervise the preparation of financial statements and periodically report to the owners on the status of the property, occupancy rates, dates of lease expirations, and other matters.

Often, property managers negotiate contracts for janitorial, security, grounds keeping, trash removal, and other services. When contracts are awarded competitively, managers solicit bids from several contractors and recommend to the owners which bid to accept. They monitor the performance of contractors and investigate and resolve complaints from residents and tenants when services are not properly provided. Managers also purchase supplies and equipment for the property and make arrangements with specialists for repairs that cannot be handled by regular property maintenance staff.

In addition to these duties, property managers must understand and comply with provisions of legislation, such as the Americans with Disabilities Act and the Federal Fair Housing Amendment Act, as well as local fair housing laws. They must ensure that their renting and advertising practices are not discriminatory and that the property itself complies with all of the local, State, and Federal regulations and building codes.

Starting out you may retain some of the functions and contract the other services to a property management firm. Property managers may not be as expensive as you'd think. It is worth investigating what the help of a property manager can do for your business.

We looked at a wide range of topics related to obtaining properties for the long haul. The average investor cannot be in this business without managing a tenant or rental property at some point. By understanding the state laws, attracting good, qualified tenants, and entering into the appropriate agreement, an investor can have much success and prosperity as a landlord.

POWER PLAY #9

Play to Win: Playing Smart with Taxes and Exchanges

Take it to where you want it to go!

Once you've bought your first investment the fears of the tax man usually start creeping in. Did I save all my documentation? What's deductible? What's depreciable? One of the best benefits of investing in real estate is that in the federal, state and local tax laws are techniques and practices that an investor can use to legally defer her taxes for an indefinite amount of time. To fully take advantage of the laws that would apply to you, it is imperative to understand the tax rules regarding real estate.

I don't expect that this Chapter will provide you with every answer that you might have, especially as your real estate portfolio grows. I do suggest, however, that you consult an accountant or tax attorney. This Chapter will give you a foundation of information that you should understand and some scenarios that may require more advanced assistance.

Taxation becomes most relevant when you own and manage real estate as well as upon the sale of a property. Let's look at both areas.

Owning and Managing Real Estate

When owning and managing real estate, the investor is able to take advantage of many deductions from property. Some of those deductions are as follows:

Deductions of purchase costs
Expenses associated with operating the business
Depreciation allowances provided by the Federal Government

Purchase Costs

Many of the costs associated with acquiring the property are tax deductible the year you purchase the property. Some those deductions are as follows:

Liability Insurance
Property tax Pro-rations
Some Closing Costs
Prepaid interest on the loan
Title Insurance fees
Escrow totals
Other fees charged by lender or escrow company

Be careful with trying to write off all Closing Costs. The rule is that loan fees and points to secure the loan should be deducted over a period of time. This was not always the rule and became the rule after abuse. Be sure to check with your tax professional prior to writing off things regarding purchase costs on your taxes. You don't want to leave any potential deductions off.

Expenses to Operate

Throughout the year, there will be many expenses that you will incur as an investor. These expenses are usually deductible. Sometimes you may wonder if the expense is truly an expense or a capital item. If the expense was incurred fixing a problem or maintaining the value of the building, it is typically deductible. Some of these deductible items include:
Utilities
Advertising
Management fees
License and City Fees
Real Estate Taxes
Insurance
Interest on Loans
Mechanical Repairs
Vehicle expenses
Other expenses

When expenses will increase the value of the property or replace an existing part of the property, these expenses are considered capital expenditures. These expenses are also depreciated over time. According to the IRS, capital expenditures can be depreciated over the time that the contribute to the properties usefulness. Items considered capital expenses are as follows:

Additions to the Building
Complete Roof or new plumbing or electrical system
New Carpeting or new flooring
New windows
Any major repair such as new siding, new driveway, etc.
Major appliances (furnace,etc.)

Some things that are not deductible are is the mortgage payment for the property. When you pay down your principal balance, you are using the income provided by the tenants to cover the mortgage payment. This is not considered a personal expense if you have a cash-flow property. You cannot deduct the principal payment because it is going towards the real estate loan and in fact is paying down the loan. This is broken down on the interest statement that you will receive from your bank at the end of the year to do your taxes.

Selling Real Estate

When it's time to sell the real estate, you should understand how Capital Gains and Exchanges work.

Capital Gains

The tax owed when you sell a property is called capital gains taxes. It is simply your tax responsibility for the profit you've earned on the property. Many people get capital gains confused because the rule changes if you live in a property and earn gains versus if you own it as an investor. Once you invest in a property outside of your main owner occupant home, you are going to be responsible for capital gains if you make a profit on the sale of the real estate. Some of the components of calculating capital gains are as follows:

Final Sale Price—The price the buyer pays for the property
Adjusted Sale Price—The price after all costs are deducted
Cost Basis—The original cost of the property plus Capital Expenses
Adjusted Cost Basis—The cost basis minus the depreciation that you've claimed

The calculations are pretty simple.

1. Take the Final Sale price minus the costs to sale and you will get the Adjusted Sale Price.

2. Take the cost basis plus the capital expenses minus depreciation and you get the Adjusted Cost Basis.

3. Take the Adjusted Sale Price minus the Adjusted Cost Basis and you get the Capital Gain.

Calculating Capital Gains

Calculation #1	Calculation #2	Calculation #3
Final Sale Price	Cost Basis	Adjusted Sale Price
Minus Sale Costs	Plus Capital Expenses	Minus Adjusted Cost Base
Equal Adjusted Sale Price	Minus Depreciation	CAPITAL GAIN
	Equal Adjusted Cost Basis	

Let's look at an example of how this may work. Assume we purchased a duplex on Sherman Street for $120,000. We've owned this property for 5 years and each year took $4000 for depreciation for each year for a total of $20,000. We added new siding for $5,000 and a new furnace for $2000. We can sell this property for $205,000 with expenses of $10,000 to sell it. Let's plug this information in.

Calculating Capital Gains

205,000 (Final Sale Price)	$120,000 (Cost Basis)	$195,000 (Adj. Sales Price)
-10,000 (Sale Costs)	+7,000 (Capital Expenses)	-$107,000 (Adj. Cost Basis)
$195,000 (Adjusted Sale price)	-20,000 (Depreciation)	$88,000 (Capital Gain)

	$107,000 (Adjusted Cost Basis)	

The tax bill on $88,000 could really hurt. Fortunately for investors, the government has developed what they call exchanges. These exchanges are a way to defer and reduce tax liability.

Understanding the 1031 Exchange

The 1031 Exchange is an important and necessary technique to know, use, and understand in your real estate career. The IRS tax-deferred exchange allows investors the opportunity to build your equity and at the same time defer your taxes. Sounds almost too good to be true...The IRS looks at this opportunity as a way to create an eventual win-win for both parties. By helping you to build your equity, the IRS knows that eventually you will have to sell and when you do, you will most likely owe a larger tax bill than when you started. It's an incentive to keep you investing. Without it, an investor pays taxes every time they move from one investment property to another.

Basically, the IRS is your ally by allowing you to roll the taxes you owe into a bigger property. You basically are trading up into a larger property. The 1031 does not forgive you of the taxes you owe but basically allows you to defer that payment.

Some key points to be familiar with when using this technique are as follows:

Trade for Like-Kind—You have to trade a property for a similar type of property. For example if you own a 2 flat rental house, you must trade for another income producing property. You cannot trade up for your dream house on the lake. You can trade for a better duplex, a multi family, or an office building as long as it's an investment property.
Trade Up-The property has to be for a property that has greater value than the first property. You can't trade up into a cheaper property.
You can't receive any cash or mortgage relief or thing of value from the transaction.

There are three types of 1031 tax-deferred exchanges. They are as follows:
The Straight Exchange
The Delayed Exchange
The Three Party Exchange

The Straight Exchange

A straight exchange is when one property is just traded with another property. You take my duplex, I'll take yours. This is rare because most investment property owners want to either trade up or get out.

The Delayed Exchange

When you sell your main home, and you have lived there for two out of the past five years before it is sold, our tax laws provide you with a tax break. As a single person you can exclude up to $250,000 of any gain you have made and up to $500,000 if you are married filing jointly.

The delayed exchange for investors is also known as the Starker Exchange. This type of exchange is named after Mr. T.J. Starker. Starker defeated the IRS when they went all the way to the Supreme Court on a tax deferred exchange case.

Currently, the capital gains tax rate is between 5-28%. But for our purposes, we'll use 15 percent. This is the average rate and a lower rate for an average income earner. Some people may not want to become landlords or continue to be a landlord over a period of time, and you may want to just pay the tax. Before you do so, however, you should give serious consideration to the exchange provisions contained in the Internal Revenue Code 1031 as far as exchanges. You must follow the rules.

An overview of the rules is as follows:
1. The property transferred is called relinquished property and the exchanged property is called replacement property. This property should be "property held for productive use in trade, in business or for investment." Neither of these properties can be your primary home unless have moved into a new house and no longer occupy this house. Language is important because it will help you refer to each house in the appropriate manner.
2. There is an exchange of property. The IRS wants to ensure that a transaction that is called an exchange. This is not a purchase or sale.
3. The replacement property must be of "like kind." Like kind is usually referred to as use. Real estate for real estate is okay. A farm can be exchanged for an office building if it has similar use.

After you've determined what type of exchange you are in you will want to determine if it is best to exchange or just do a sale and pay the taxes. You should know what the tax would be for a straight sale versus the benefit of a starker exchange. You can have your tax professional or accountant prepare these numbers for you. It may be better to just cash out.

One disadvantage for a starter investor to do a like-kind exchange, if you have a ton of money tied up in the property, is that your profit will be deferred until you sell the replacement property. However, you should understand that the cost basis of the new property in most cases will be the basis of the old property. Your real estate attorney or accountant can help you with this.

When doing a Starker Exchange, consider the following rules
1. The replacement property must be identified before the 45th day after the day on which the original (relinquished) property is transferred.
2. The replacement property (or properties) must be purchased no later than 180 days after the taxpayer transfers his original property, or the due date (with any extension) of the taxpayer's return of the tax imposed for the year in which the transfer is made. These are very important time limitations, which should be noted on your calendar when you first enter into a 1031 exchange. They are mandated by Congress and cannot be extended by even one day.
3. In 1989, Congress added two additional technical restrictions. First, property located in the United States cannot be exchanged for property outside the United States.
4. If property received in a like-kind exchange between related persons is disposed of within two years after the date of the last transfer, the original exchange will not qualify for non-recognition of gain.
Many of these restrictions were determined in May of 1991 by the Internal Revenue Service when they adopted final regulations which clarified many of the issues. Some additional rules determined were as follows:
Partnerships no longer had a "like-kind" interest for exchanges
An identification Statement describing the replacement property must be completed by midnight on the 45th day
The taxpayer must receive this property by the 180th day.
A third party accommodator must be used to facilitate the exchange. Check out companies like www.starker.com.

I am by no means an expert on IRS codes, so I advise you to consult a tax attorney to understand using Starkers and other exchanges. The result of a bad exchange deal could be more costly than just paying the capital gains. Sometimes paying the taxes may have a simpler outcome than trying to enter into exchanges and other unknown territory. There is enough that could potentially trip you up and you don't want the IRS to be one of them. When in doubt seek legal advice or just pay the taxes.
The Three Party Exchange

Less complicated than the Starker is the three-party exchange. This exchange is simply a 3-way trade can occur so each investor wins.

This might work as follows:

Janet owns a four unit building and wants to upgrade to a mixed use office building with apartments on top.

Mesha owns a mixed use office building with apartments but wants to cash out pay the taxes and move to Atlanta.

Christy is new to investing and wants to buy a four unit building that Janet owns.

Janet and Mesha can enter an exchange deal in which Janet gets the office building and Mesha takes the four-unit. Mesha in a separate deal, enters an agreement with Christy to sell her the 4 unit after Mesha and Janet are finished with their exchange. Christy pays for the 4 unit and obtains title from Mesha. All these transactions are contingent on the circle working.

Wow! So what happens. At the end of the deal, Christy starts her investing career with the new 4 unit and begins her wealth building plan, Janet gets the mixed use with apartments on top and increases her cash flow, and Mesha is partying in Atlanta with the cash from the deal. Mesha doesn't have to pay any taxes on the 4-unit because it is sold for the same price at which it was taken in trade.

Playing To Win

When playing any game, I play to win. I want to be the best I can be and get the most out of that experience. If your goal in real estate investing is to have financial freedom, residual income, life changing wealth, a huge part of your success is the team that is built around you.

Building a real estate brain team will help to fill in the missing parts of your knowledge base as you build your skills. To be successful in real estate investing, you need the following skills and abilities:

The ability to identify, locate, and acquire good "deals"

The ability to negotiate a below market price for your property

The ability to finance real estate deals

The ability to renovate and upgrade your property

The ability to understand and price repair costs

The ability to attract, manage and keep good tenants

The ability to sell and profit from your investment

The ability to protect yourself from tax & insurance issues

The ability to acquire, manage, and maintains a real estate portfolio

The ability to improve your skills and strengthen your brain team

That's an intimidating list. A list that no one woman or man I know can tackle alone. Even if you personally possessed all of those skills and abilities, who would want to do all the work of acquiring, managing, and building a real estate business. Our ability to grow will depend on our ability to expand our knowledge base and increase our capacity to handle more investment ventures. This only happens by sharing the wealth and bringing in experts to assist in achieving your one ultimate goal.

Some of the team members you may want to employ are as follows:
A Real Estate Broker
A Tax Attorney
An accountant
A Real Estate Attorney
An appraiser
A plethora of contractors
A management company
A loan officer
An insurance agent
A business partner

This list could go on an on. In order to get started, you don't need all these people at once but at certain points, they may come in and provide sound advice in their area. Use them for their expertise, we do not have time to become an expert in every tax law, however, it is wise to know that they exist and what implications the laws have on your business.

I am notorious for trying to do everything, know everything, be everybody. Trust me—it doesn't work. Let them help you. Learn from them, lean on them, and let them show you how to build wealth from their expertise.

Final Words

The Power to Play

Anyone can be a real estate investor and anyone can make money doing it. We've discussed 9 simple power plays that anyone can implement. Anyone can but not everyone will. Will you?

The resources are available to assist you with a successful real estate career are plentiful. Get the information and get moving. As I drive around my town, I look at houses that have sold through years and reflect on the prices then and the current value, now. If I'd only moved faster and not been afraid, how would my life be different?

For everything there is a divine season. Step into your season and let increasing market values and cashflow enter into your life. I know you may read in the paper and the magazines that the bubble has burst, values are falling, and interest rates are high. Remember the formula for success and you never again have to worry if the market is up or down, hot or cold because you will come out on top. I wish you Godspeed in your endeavors. I know real estate is a big purchase but dare to think big to live a big life.

We started with Why? We're ending with Why not?

There are so many reasons to do something that could change and empower your life. Maybe its freedom for yourself or if not for yourself then for your children. The answers are simple. The process is pretty simple too. Don't let fear leave you in the same place. Get out there and do something. If you don't do something then you must not want anything. If it's help you need then get help. There are experts in every field that can help you.

If you've got bad credit, work on it. If you've got no money, great, look for a no money down program or housing program. I've never seen an opportunity out there for so many people and many just don't take advantage. If you don't own a home, then first you must do that. Buy your own home then don't stop.

There is absolutely no reason that you can't buy your own home. It may take some time. It may take some effort but I know it can be done. It can be done by people with bad credit. It can be done by people who just started working. It can be done by single mothers. Just do it. Don't let finances stop you from believing in yourself and reaching towards your dreams. The ownership of real estate can be so positive in your life. Starting your wealth building process by investing in real estate is simple and practical and obtainable. Why not? You really can't lose. Just get started and you'll see the future looks pretty bright. Embrace your financial freedom.

Appendix

Useful Real Estate Forms
Landlord Forms
Purchase Forms

Residential Lease Agreement

THIS LEASE AGREEMENT is made and entered into this _____ day of __
_____, 20 ____, by and between _____
hereinafter referred to as "Landlord" and _____,
hereinafter referred to as "Tenant".

Landlord leases to Tenant and Tenant leases from Landlord, upon the terms and conditions contained herein, the dwelling located at _____
_____ for the period commencing on the _____
day of _____,20 ____, and thereafter until the _____ day of _____
___, 20 ____, at which time this Lease Agreement shall automatically renew each year unless terminated in writing. The Tenant is required to give the Landlord in writing a notice 1 month (30 days) in advance of his/her moving. Notice must be given on the first day of a month. If notice is given after the first day of the month, the 1 month (30 day) notice will not start until the following month. (The notice must be one full calendar month starting on the first day of a month.) Rent may be increased at any time after first year and the security deposit can not be used for rent.

Tenant shall pay as rent the sum of $ _____ per month, due and payable monthly, in advance, no later than 5:00 p.m. by the forth day of every month. Tenant further agrees to pay a late charge of $_____ for each day rent is not received after the forth of the month to the Landlord regardless of the cause, including dishonored checks, time being of the essence. An additional Service Charge of $_____ will be paid to Landlord for all dishonored checks.

As an incentive to Tenant to make rent payments before the first of the month and for being responsible for all minor maintenance of the premises, a pre-payment discount in the amount of $_____ may be deducted from the above rental amount each month. Said discount will be forfeited if Tenant fails to perform as stated above.

Tenant agrees to use said dwelling as living quarters only for _____ adults and _____children, namely:

_____
and to pay $50.00 each month for each other person who shall occupy the premises in any capacity.

Tenant agrees to accept the property in its current condition and to return it in "moving-in clean" condition, or to pay a special cleaning charge of $185.00 upon vacating the premises. The carpets are to be professionally cleaned. If you prefer that we have the carpets cleaned for you the charge will be billed to you. Carpet cleaning cost are in addition to cleaning charge.

PETS ARE NOT ALLOWED WITHOUT WRITTEN PERMISSION FROM LANDLORD. As additional rent, Tenant agrees to pay a non-refundable pet fee of $10.00 per month for each pet. All pets on the property not registered under this Lease shall be presumed to be strays and will be disposed of by the appropriate agency as prescribed by law. A Pet Agreement, if applicable, is attached hereto as Exhibit "B", and incorporated herein by reference. PET NAMES AND DESCRIPTION: _____

Tenant agrees not to assign this Lease, nor to sublet any portion of the property, nor to allow any other person to live therein other than as named in paragraph 4 above without first obtaining written permission from Landlord and paying the appropriate surcharge. Further, it is agreed that covenants contained in this Lease, once breached, cannot afterward be performed, and that unlawful detainer proceedings may be commenced at once, without notice to Tenant.

Should any provision of this Lease be found to be invalid or unenforceable, the remainder of the Lease shall not be affected thereby and each term and provision herein shall be valid and enforceable to the fullest extent permitted by law.

All rights given to Landlord by this Lease shall be cumulative to any other laws which might exist or come into being. Any exercise or failure to exercise by Landlord of any right shall not act as a waiver of any other rights. No statement or promise of Landlord or his agent as to tenancy, repairs, alterations, or other terms and conditions shall be binding unless reduced to writing and signed by Landlord.

Tenant will be responsible for payment of all utilities, garbage, water and sewer charges, telephone, gas, association fees or other bills incurred during the term of this Lease. Tenant specifically authorizes Landlord to deduct amounts of any unpaid bills from the Security deposit upon termination of this Agreement.

No rights of storage are given by this Agreement. Landlord shall not be liable for any loss of Tenant's property by fire, theft, breakage, burglary, or otherwise, nor for any accidental damage to persons or property in or about the leased premises resulting from electrical failure, water, rain, windstorm, etc., which may cause issue or flow into or from any part of said premises or improvements, including pipes, gas lines, sprinklers, or electrical connections, whether caused by the negligence of Landlord, Landlord's employees, contractors, agents, or by any other cause whatsoever. Tenant hereby agrees to make no claim for any such damages or loss against Landlord. Tenant shall purchase renter's insurance. _____ is to be named as additional Insured

IMPROVEMENTS TO PROPERTY—Any improvements to the property made by tenant inside or outside must not be removed without written permission from the property manger. This includes landscaping, scrubs, flowers, walkways, out buildings such as storage sheds and play-houses, etc. Any interior improvements the tenant may have made to the property must also remain. Improvements such as but not limited to the following are installation of ceiling fans, book shelves, shelving, light fixtures, etc.

Any removal of Landlord's property without express written permission from the Landlord shall constitute abandonment and surrender of the premises and termination by the resident of this Agreement. Landlord may take immediate possession, exclude Tenant from property and store all Tenant's possessions at Tenant's expense pending reimbursement in full for Landlord's loss and damages.

Landlord has the right of emergency access to the leased premises at any time and access during reasonable hours to inspect the property or to show property to a prospective tenant or buyer. In the event that the property is sold, the lease/rental agreement between Landlord and Tenant is canceled on the date the new owner takes possession of property. Tenant has thirty days to vacate the property or sign new lease with new owner at new owner's option.

Tenant agrees to pay a Security Deposit of $ _____ to bind Tenant's pledge of full compliance with the terms of this agreement. NOTE: SECURITY DEPOSIT MAY NOT BE USED TO PAY RENT! Any damages not previously reported as required in paragraph 25, will be repaired at Tenant's expense.

Release of the SECURITY DEPOSIT, at the Option of the Landlord is subject to the provisions below.

A. The full term of the Agreement has been completed.

B. No damage to the premises, buildings, grounds is evident.

C. The entire dwelling, appliances, closets, and cupboards are clean and free from insects, the refrigerator is defrosted and clean, The range is to be clean including the racks and broiler pan, all windows are to be clean inside and outside, all debris and rubbish have been removed from the property, carpets have been commercially cleaned and left clean and odorless.

D. All unpaid charges have been paid including late charges, visitor charges, pet charges, delinquent rents, etc. WATER BILL MUST BE PAID IN FULL AND COPY OF PAID FINAL BILL SENT TO LANDLORD.

E. All keys have been returned.

F. A forwarding address for Tenant has been left with the Landlord. Within thirty (30) days after termination of the occupancy, the Landlord will mail the balance of the deposit to the address provided by Tenant in the names of all signatories hereto; or at the Option of the Landlord will impose a claim on the deposit and so notify the Tenant.

G. It is the tenant's responsibility to call, make arrangements, and be at residence to let meter readers in for final reading on gas, electric, and water. If Landlord has to do this, there is a $50 charge for each utility.

The acceptance by Landlord of partial payments of rent due shall not, under any circumstances, constitute a waiver of Landlord, nor affect any notice or legal proceeding in unlawful detainer theretofore given or commenced under state law. Acceptance of partial rent due or late payments does not create a custom nor constitute a continuing waiver of the obligation to pay on time. No payment by the tenant or receipt by the landlord of any amount of the monthly rent herein stipulated shall be deemed to be other than on account of the stipulated rent, nor shall any endorsement on any check or any letter accompanying such payment of rent be deemed an accord and satisfaction, but the landlord may accept such a partial payment without prejudice to his rights to collect the balance of such rent.

If Tenant leaves said premises unoccupied for 15 days while rent is due and unpaid, Landlord is granted the right hereunder to take immediate possession thereof and to exclude Tenant there from; removing all Tenant's property contained therein and placing it into storage at Tenant's expense.

Payment of rent may be made by check until the first check is returned unpaid. Regardless of cause, no additional payments may afterwards be made by check. Rent must then be made by cashier's check, money order or certified check.

Rent may be mailed through the United States Postal Service at Tenant's risk. Any rents lost in the mail will be treated as if unpaid until received by Landlord.

Tenant agrees, without protest, to reimburse Landlord for all actual and reasonable expenses incurred by way of Tenant's violation of any term or provision of this lease, including, but not limited to $10.00 for each Notice to Pay, Notice to Quit or other notice mailed or delivered by Landlord to Tenant due to Tenant's non-payment of rent, all court costs and attorney's fees and all costs of collection. Both Landlord and Tenant waive trial by jury and agree to submit to the personal jurisdiction and venue of a court of subject matter jurisdiction located in _____ County, State of _____. In such event, no action shall be entertained by said court or any court of competent jurisdiction if filed more than one year subsequent to the date the cause(s) of action accrued.

Tenant agrees to accept said dwelling and all of the furnishings and appliances therein as being in good and satisfactory condition unless a written statement of any objections is delivered to Landlord within three (3) days after resident takes possession. Tenant agrees that failure to file such statement shall be conclusive proof that there were no defects in the property. Tenant agrees not to permit any damage to the premises during the period of this agreement to woodwork, floors, walls, furnishings, fixtures, appliances, windows, screens, doors, lawns, landscaping, fences, plumbing, electrical, air conditioning and heating, and mechanical systems. Tenant specifically agrees that he will be responsible for, and agrees to pay for, any damage done by rain, wind, or hail caused by leaving windows open; overflow of water or stoppage of waste pipes, breakage of glass, damage to screens, deterioration of lawns and landscaping whether caused by drought, abuse or neglect. Tenant agrees not to park or store a motorhome, recreational vehicle or trailer of any type on the premises.

Tenant's obligations are as follows:

A. Take affirmative action to insure that nothing is done which might place Landlord in violation of applicable building, housing, zoning, and health codes and regulations.

B. Keep the dwelling clean and sanitary, removing garbage and trash as it accumulates, maintaining plumbing in good working order to prevent stoppages and leakage of plumbing fixtures, faucets, pipes, etc.

C. Operate all electrical, plumbing, sanitary, heating, ventilating, air conditioning, and other appliances in a reasonable, safe manner.

D. Assure that property belonging to Landlord is safeguarded against damage, destruction, loss, removal, or theft.

E. Conduct himself, his family, friends, guests, visitors in a manner which will not disturb others.

F. Allow the Landlord or his agent access to the premises for the purpose of inspection, repairs, or to show the property to someone else at reasonable hours, and to specifically authorize unannounced access anytime rent is late, or this Agreement is terminated or for pest control, maintenance estimates, serving legal notices, or emergencies.

G. Comply with all provisions of this Agreement, particularly with respect to paying the rent on time and caring for the property. Tenant warrants that he/she will meet the above conditions in every respect, and acknowledges that failure to perform the obligations herein stipulated will be considered grounds for termination of this Agreement and loss of all deposits.

No additional locks will be installed on any door without written permission from the Landlord. Landlord is to be provided duplicate keys for all locks so installed at Tenant's expense within 24 hours of installation of said locks.

Tenant agrees to install and maintain a telephone, and to furnish the Landlord the telephone number and/or any changes thereof within three (3) days of its installation.

In the event repairs are needed beyond the competence of the Tenant, Tenant is urged to contact the Landlord. Tenant is offered the discount as an incentive to make his own decisions on repairs to the property and to allow Landlord to rent the property without the need to employ professional management. Therefore, as much as possible, Tenant should refrain from contacting the Landlord or his agent except for emergencies, or for expensive repairs. Such involvement by the Landlord or his agent will result in the loss of the discount and/or deductible.

Tenant warrants that any work or repairs performed by him will be undertaken only if he is competent and qualified to perform it. Tenant will be totally responsible for all activities to assure that work is done in a safe manner which will meet all the applicable codes and statutes. Tenant further warrants that he will be accountable for any mishaps and/or accidents resulting from such work, and will hold the Landlord free from harm, litigation, or claims of any other person.

Tenant is responsible for all plumbing repairs including faucets, leaks, stopped up pipes, frozen pipes, water damage, and bathroom caulking.

Appliances or furniture in the unit at date of lease per the attached Exhibit "A", are loaned, not leased to Tenant. Maintenance of appliances or furniture is the responsibility of Tenant who will keep them in good repair.

Tenant is responsible for all glass, screen, and storm door repairs.

No money is to be deducted by Tenant from rent payment for any reason without express written permission of Landlord.

Regardless of assignment of responsibility, Tenant agrees to be responsible for the first $75.00 of any repair or maintenance required on the major systems of the property for the term of the lease. This deductible applies per occurrence.

Tenant accepts entirely the responsibility for recharging air conditioner compressor and the cleaning of furnace or replacement of furnace filters.

Smoke Detectors have been installed and are in operable condition in the following places. _____

Tenant initials _____. From this time on you will be required to maintain the smoke detectors. Any new batteries are your responsibility. If you have any questions about the smoke detectors, you should call us promptly.

I/We, the undersigned, have personally checked the smoke alarms in the unit which is provided and find it/them to be in working order. I/We understand that the law requires me/us to maintain the alarm/s and keep fresh batteries in the mechanism. Tenant's failure to do so absolves the Landlord, or agent from any responsibility for losses due to my/our non-compliance with the law or malfunction of the alarm.

Tenant signature _____ Date _____

NO WATER BEDS PERMITTED WITHOUT WRITTEN PERMISSION.

All parties agree that termination of this Agreement prior to termination date will constitute breach of the tenancy and all Security Deposits and one full month's rent shall be forfeited in favor of Landlord as liquidated damages plus you will be charged the cost of restoring the property to rental condition plus advertising and rent loss incurred until the new resident moves in. Your liability for rent loss is limited to thirty (30) days after restoration is complete.

Properties built before and during the late sixties and early seventies may have had lead based products and asbestos products used in them. These products were considered to be safe at the time they were used, just as the building products used today are considered safe for home construction. Only the test of time will show which products are or are not safe to use. Having read the above, the tenant signs the lease below with the full understanding that these conditions may be present in this property. The tenant and all parties associated with this property relieves the owner, property manager, and any of his agents from any responsibilities for these conditions regardless of when or how these conditions were caused.

You also acknowledge receiving the EPA Booklet "Protect Your Family From Lead In Your Home"

X _____

Tenant Signature Date

X _____

Tenant Signature Date

From time to time, owner may be represented by an agent who will carry identification.

In this Agreement the singular number where used will also include the plural, the masculine gender will also include the feminine, the term Landlord will include, Owner or Lessor; and the term Tenant(s) will include Resident, Lessee or Renter.

Unless specifically disallowed by law, should litigation arise hereunder, service of process therefore may be obtained through certified mail, return receipt requested; the parties hereto waiving any and all rights they may have to object to the method by which service was perfected.

TENANT agrees to send all notices to Landlord or Property Manager in writing by certified mail, return receipt requested. This is the only form of notice permitted in a court hearing as evidence of notice given.

The Tenant was asked if he/she could speak, read and understand English. He/she was told that signing below would indicate that they understood what they were signing and that he/she did speak and read English.

YOU SHOULD READ AND UNDERSTAND THIS LEASE, IT IS A LEGAL AND BINDING CONTRACT.

Signing below means you have read the Lease, are in full agreement with it and have received a copy of the contract.

ACCEPTED THIS _____ DAY OF _____19 _____,

at _____.

(Address, City and State)

_____

Tenant 1

_____   _____

Tenant 2   Landlord, Property manager or Agent

EXHIBIT "A"

The following appliances and/or furniture are on loan to Tenant for the period of Tenant's rental agreement or lease on the following basis: Tenant agrees, by the signing of this agreement, that all appliances and/or furniture herein listed are accepted by Tenant, individually, as being in good working order or condition. Tenant agrees to maintain said appliances and/or furniture in good working order at his expense. If tenant fails to pay rent by the fifth day of the month, the landlord/manager or his representative may enter building and remove appliances or furniture belonging to Landlord without giving tenant advance notice.

APPLIANCES AND/OR FURNITURE

	Furniture Description	Appliance Number or Item	Condition	Location
1				
2				
3				
4				
5				
6				
7				

8				
9				
10				
11				
12				
13				
14				
15				
16				

Tenant: _____

Date: _____

EXHIBIT "B"
PET AGREEMENT
Date: _____ (Addendum to Lease Agreement)

This agreement is attached to and forms a part of the Lease Agreement dated _____ between _____ _____, Landlord, and _____, Tenant(s).

Tenants desire to keep a pet named _____ ____ and described as _____ in the dwelling they occupy under the rental agreement or lease referred to above, and because this agreement specifically prohibits keeping pets without the Landlord's permission, Tenants agree to the following terms and conditions in exchange for this permission:

Tenants agree to keep their pet under control at all times.

Tenants agree to keep their pet restrained, but not tethered, when it is outside their dwelling.

Tenants agree not to leave their pet unattended for any unreasonable periods.

Tenants agree to dispose of their pet's droppings properly and quickly.

Tenants agree to keep pet from causing any annoyance or discomfort to others and will remedy immediately any complaints made through the Landlord or his agent.

Tenants agree to get rid of their pet's offspring within eight weeks of birth.

Tenants agree to pay immediately for any damage, loss, or expense caused by their pet, and in addition, they will add $ _____ to their Security Deposit, any of which may be used for cleaning, repairs, or delinquent rent when Tenants vacate.

Tenants agree that Landlord reserves the right to revoke permission to keep the pet should Tenants break this agreement.

Tenant agrees to pay an additional $ _____ in rent per month per pet.

_____

TENANT

_____

Month-to-Month Lease Agreement

Date:_____, 19___

RECEIPT IS HEREBY ACKNOWLEDGED by_____
_____ hereinafter Called Management, from_____
_____ hereinafter called Resident, the sum of $_____
for the first month's rent of the premises owned by said Management and located
at_____ hereinafter called premises,
said premises the Management hereby agrees to rent to said Resident on a
month-to-month basis at a rental of $_____ per month, payable in
advance on the___ day of each and every succeeding calendar month.

In considered hereof and of the use or occupancy of the said premises, Resident
agrees:

1. To maintain said premises in a clean, orderly, and law abiding manner and to
keep the yards thereof free of weeds, debris, and/or material that may become
unsightly or a detriment to the appearance of said premises. Management
shall have the right to enter and inspect said premises at any and all reasonable
times.

2. No alterations or redecorating of any kind to the dwelling shall be made
without the prior written consent of Management.

3. To pay for all utility service furnished to the property.

4. To pay the cost of all repairs for any damage done to said premises and the
cost of any cleaning up of said premises which Management may consider necessary.

5. No birds, animals, or other pets shall be kept on the premises without the
knowledge and written consent from Management; any consent, so given may
be withdrawn, if, in the opinion of Management, such bird, animal, or other pet
constitutes a nuisance, causes complaint from neighbors, or adversely affects
the normal maintenance of the property.

6. Not to let or sublet the whole or any part of the premises to anyone for any
purpose whatsoever without prior written permission from Management, and

the number of persons to occupy said premises shall not exceed without written permission from Management.

7. To give thirty days written notice by registered mail to Management prior to vacating said premises and to permit prospective tenants the opportunity of reasonable inspection.

8. To clean up said premises upon vacating and restore said premises to the same condition they are now in, reasonable wear and tear and damage by the elements excepted.

9. That the violation of any of the covenants of this agreement or the nonpayment of any rent due and unpaid shall be sufficient cause for eviction from said premises upon three (3) days written notice thereof by registered mail or by personal service. If suit be brought to collect rent or damages, to cause eviction from said premises, or to collect the costs of repairs to or cleaning of said premises, Resident agrees to pay all costs of such action, including reasonable attorney fees as may be fixed by the Court. No waiver by Management at any time of any of the terms of this agreement shall be deemed as a subsequent waiver of the same, nor of the strict and prompt performance thereof by the Resident.

10. All rent shall be paid at the office of_____,
or any other place designated by Management. Each party hereto acknowledges receipt of a copy of this agreement.

_____

Signed_____
Management Resident

By_____
Signed_____
Resident

Rules And Regulations

Care and Maintenance of the Apartment

No birds, cats, dogs or other animals shall be maintained in or about the premises.

Ashes, garbage, sweepings, dirt, litter or refuse shall be wrapped and deposited in garbage bins for that purpose.

Water shall not be left running in bathroom, kitchen or elsewhere in the premises and all leaks shall be immediately reported to the Resident Manager or Owner.

Signs shall not be posted in or about the demised premises or building.

Toilets, sinks and wash-basins are to be used only for the purpose for which they are intended, and no dust, rubbish, litter, coffee grounds, tea leaves, egg shells, or any garbage are to be put into same.

No piano or other musical instruments including radios shall be permitted before 8:30 am or later than 10:30 pm if other Tenants are bothered by it.

No credit will be given for repairs made by Tenants.

Tenants may not drive nails in walls without permission from Resident Manager. Only small picture-hanging brads may be used. "Stick on" hangers may not be used on painted surfaces.

Use of washing machines and dryers within the apartment units is prohibited before 8:30 am or after 10:30 pm. Tenant shall not use bathtubs, basin nor kitchen sink for laundry purposes. Damage to the plumbing equipment resulting from this or any other abnormal use of this equipment must be repaired at the expense of the Tenant.

When individual heating equipment, electric range, refrigerator or other automatic equipment is included in the rental unit for the sole use of the occupant, such equipment shall be kept in a state comparable to that which it was in at the time of occupancy by the Tenant.

Use of Halls, Roof, Common Areas, etc.

Children are positively not allowed to play in corridors, entrance halls or on the roof or in the basement.

No windowsills, fire escapes, ledges or light shafts shall be used for storage purposes. No public halls or passageways shall, in any way be obstructed by packages, boxes or otherwise.

All furniture, supplies, carts, material, etc.; shall be received and delivered via the rear or basement entrance.

Tenants are not permitted access to the roof except in case of emergency.

Inoperable cars must be removed from parking areas and will be subject to being towed at Tenant's expense.

Tenants are not allowed to work on their cars in the parking areas. Tenant shall not have more than one (1) car in the parking lot without prior approval.

Use of Laundry

Use of laundry includes the facilities only.

Laundry room may be used only during the time allotted by the Resident Manager.

The Management reserves the right to refuse Tenant the use of the laundry and storeroom and all other building facilities for failure to comply with laws and ordinances governing safety, health and sanitation.

Use of the laundry and its facilities shall be limited to the washing of the usual personal and household articles. No cleaning with flammable materials is permitted.

Use of the laundry room may be denied to any Tenant who causes unpleasantness therein or who disregards the rules pertaining thereto. The Owner or Agent will not be responsible for any articles lost, stolen or damaged on these premises.

The Owner/Agent reserve the right to make such additional rules and regulations, as they may deem necessary.

I HAVE READ AND UNDERSTAND THE ABOVE.

_____   _____
Tenant   Date

_____   _____
Tenant   Date

Move-In/Move-Out Check ListProperty address:_____

(1) This form is to be completed by owner/manager. Resident is encouraged to be present during inspection. (2) This form is for the protection of our residents. Any shortage of fixtures or appliances, damage to property, unusual wear to the property will be charged to the tenant.

Number of keys given to tenant: Date:

	MOVE IN	MOVE OUT	CHARGES
KITCHEN cabinets condition			
cabinets clean			
REFRIGERATOR clean			
2 ice cube trays			
2 crispers & tops			
light bulb			
ice caddie			
STOVE clean & working			
oven racks clean			
broiler pan clean			
light bulb			
DISPOSAL clean & working			
COUNTER TOP condition			
FAN,FILTER,HOOD clean			
BATHROOM #1 clean			
SOAP DISHES, towel bars			
shower rod, paper holder			
plumbing works properly			
caulking & tile clean			
fan clean/working			
BATHROOM #2 clean			
SOAP DISHES, towel bars			
shower rod, paper holder			
plumbing works properly			
caulking & tile clean			
fan clean & working			
HEATING AND AIR COND.			
clean & working			
furnace filters			
DOORS work properly			
door knobs work			
door locks work			

WINDOWS work properly
windows clean
screens
storm windows
BROKEN/CRACKED windows
CONDITION of doors,frames
condition of woodwork
CARPETS clean yes or no
burns,tears,stains (name)
CURTAIN RODS & fixtures
BLINDS & shades
RUBBISH removed
LIGHTING fixtures & bulbs
WALLS surfaces clean
not repainted or wallpapered
VENTS & registers work
ELECTRICAL outlets work
cover plates on outlets
MIRRORS clean
SMOKE detectors work
COMMENTS: _____

_____By   signing
our name below I/we accept the aforementioned MOVE IN _ MOVE OUT
_ CHECK LIST as a part of the rental agreement and agree that it is an accurate account of the condition and contents of said premises and acknowledge receiving a copy hereof. I/we also agree to pay for any damages to the property and contents other than normal wear.
RESIDENT_____ DATE_____
MANAGER _____ DATE_____

Agreement to Lease With Option to Purchase
Parties: Buyer _____ of

_____
and
Seller, _____
of _____
In consideration of the payments, covenants, agreements and conditions herein
contained the above parties hereby agree to lease
With an option the following property:
Subject: Property Address: _____

_____
Legal Description: _____

_____
_____
_____

Personal Property included_____

_____
Personal property to be transferred at closing by bill of sale free of any encum-
brances.
Existing Loans-At time of closing buyer may elect to take title subject to the
existing loans to_____
In the amount of $_____ bearing interest rate of _____
__% payable _____ (P & I)
Or the loan will be paid off by the seller.
Loan Number_____ Date last payment made_

_____
Other Liens, back taxes, etc._____

_____
Term of lease and option _____months beginning _____

_____
Monthly Payment $_____due on the _____day of each
month beginning_____ 20____
Monthly credit toward purchase price when rent paid on time $_____
___
Purchase Price $_____, additional option consideration _____
_____to apply towards purchase price.
TERMS: Seller agrees that upon the exercise of the option they will assist in
financing by taking as part of the purchase price a note in the amount of $___

_____ with payments of $_____ beginning
_____.

MAINTENANCE: The buyers shall pay for all repairs costing less than $ 100.00 each month. Repairs costing $100 or more will be paid by the owner. Should the owner fail to make repairs to maintain the house in its current condition, the buyer may have said repairs made and receive a credit equal to 200% of the cost of the repair toward the purchase price and a full credit toward the next payment due.

SELLER'S AGREEMENT NOT TO FURTHER ENCUMBER: Sellers agree not to refinance the property, nor to modify any existing loans, nor to transfer any interest in the property during the term of this agreement.

PAYMENTS ON EXISTING LOANS, TAXES AND INSURANCE: Seller shall be responsible for paying the taxes, loan payments and for keeping the property insured for its full replacement value during the term of this agreement. In the event seller fails to make payments when due of taxes, insurance, or loan payments, buyer may elect to make said pays due payments and receive 200% of their amount credited toward the purchase price and full credit toward the next payment due the seller.

PRORATIONS: Taxes and insurance and loan interest shall be prorated as of the date of closing of the purchase.

BUYER & SELLER: agree to fully execute and place in escrow with _____
_____ instruments needed to convey title. The seller shall deposit and executed warranty deed, and copies of existing mortgages, notes, title insurance policies, and surveys. Buyer shall deposit an executed quitclaim deed which will be delivered to the seller in the event of a default by the buyer under this contract. All agree to sign an escrow agreement that will empower the escrow agent to close the transaction if all terms of the contract are met, and that will hold the agent harmless.

TRANSFER OF TITLE: In the event buyer chooses to exercise their option to purchase, they will notify the seller during the term of this agreement. Within 15 days of receipt of such notice, sellers agree to convey good and marketable title, free from all encumbrances except those that buyers wishes to take title subject to. Sellers further agree to furnish an owner's title binder within 5 days after receiving notice, showing no exceptions other than as listed above, and furnish a policy of title insurance at closing.

DAMAGES: In the event seller fails to perform, buyer will be entitled to recover all monies paid on this agreement, and may pursue all other legal remedies available. Seller will be responsible for all costs including a reasonable attorney's fee. In the event buyer fails to exercise the option, all option consideration and rents paid will be forfeited as full-liquidated damages.

RECORDING: All parties agree that this agreement or a memorandum including any parts of their agreement acceptable to the buyer may be recorded.

SUCCESSORS AND ASSIGNS & SUBLETTING: The terms and conditions of this contract shall bind all successors, heirs, administrators, executors, assigns, and those subletting.

ACCESS AND ADVERTISING: Sellers agree that the buyer may advertise the property and shall immediately have access during reasonable hours to show the property to others.

TIME IS OF THE ESSENCE IN ALL MATTERS OF THE AGREEMENT

OTHER TERMS: _____

_____

_____

_____

_____

_____

_____

_____

_____

_____

The undersigned agree to buy and sell on the above terms, have-read, fully understand and verify the above information as being correct. All parties acknowledge that this is a legally binding contract and are advised to seek the counsel of an attorney.

Sellers _____

_____

Seller's _____

_____

Buyer's _____

_____

Buyer's _____

_____

State of _____ County of _____

_____

The foregoing instrument was acknowledged before me this day of

_____

By_____

_____being

Personally known to me or who presented driver's licenses as identification.

Witness my hand and official seal.
Notary Public_____
My commission Expires_____

Personal Financial Snapshot

ASSETS

Cash $_____

Checking Accounts $_____

Savings Accounts $_____

Real Estate

Home (fair market value) $_____

Other $_____

Life Insurance

Cash Value $_____

Personal Property

Cars (market value) $_____

Furniture & Appliances $_____

Clothing & Jewelry $_____

Cameras, Tools, Art, etc. $_____

Investments

Stocks, Bonds & Mutual Funds $_____

Saving Certificates $_____

IRAs, Keoghs, 401k Plans, etc. $_____

Debts Owed to You $_____

Other Investments $_____

TOTAL ASSETS $_____

LIABILITIES

Current Bills

Charge Accounts & Credit Cards $_____

Gas, Electric, Water, Phone, etc. $_____

Child Support & Alimony $_____

Loans

Automobile $_____

Furniture & Appliances $_____

Education & Personal Loans $_____

Home Improvement $_____

Other $_____

Mortgage Principle Balance
Owed $_____

Taxes Due $_____

Insurance Premiums $_____

Other Liabilities $_____

TOTAL LIABILITIES $_____

NET WORTH (Assets minus $_____
Liabilities)

Date

Name
Address

Credit Bureau Information

Dear Sir or Madam:

I am writing to dispute information on my credit report. The items I wish to dispute are listed below and also highlighted on the attached copy of my credit report.

List Derogatory Items Here

I have contacted the creditor numerous times regarding this matter and they assure me that they show my account has a zero balance. I have returned all equipment to them and they will not issue a letter.

Please help me to resolve this matter as soon as possible. This negative mark on my credit report is affecting my ability to purchase a new home.

Thank you for investigating this matter.

Sincerely,

Your Name
Your Maiden Name or Name at time of Debt
Your Address
Your Social Security Number

Enclosures: Enclose any supporting Documentation

Property Financial Worksheet
Address:_____   First Call Date:_____
_____   Second Call Date:_____
_____   Third Call Date:_____
Owner:_____   Fourth Call Date:_____
Phone #:_____   Fifth Call Date:_____

1. Estimated after repaired value $_____
Acquisition Expenses

2. Down Payment $_____

3. Purchase Closing Cost (including
Atty., Fees, Recording, Title Ins.)   _____

4. Appraisal $_____

5. Survey $_____

6. Property Inspection $_____

7. Termite Letter $_____

8. Finder's Fee/Commission $_____

9. Contingencies/Misc. $_____

10. Total Expenses (-) $_____
Fix Up Expenses

11. Repairs Budget $_____

12. Contingencies/Misc. $_____

13. Total Fix- Up Expenses (-) $_____*
Holding Expenses

14. Payments @ _____
for _____ mos. $_____*

15. Property Tax $_____

16. Insurance $_____ *

17. Utilities $_____ *

18. Total Holding Expenses (-) $_____
Sales Expenses

19. Sales Closing Costs $_____

20. Commission $_____

21. Advertising $_____ *

22. Total Sales Expenses (-) $_____

Sales Price (10, 13, 18, 22 subtracted) $_____

Mortgage Pay-Off (-) $_____

ESTIMATED NET PROFIT $_____

CASH REQUIREMENTS
(lines 10+13+14+16+17+21) $_____

Purchase and Sale Agreement

This agreement is made this _____day of _____, 20_____

between Seller(s)_____ Social Security #_____

and Buyer _____

and or assignees. Seller agrees to sell and buyer agrees to buy the following described real property together with all improvements and fixtures and the personal property described below:

Street Address_____

Legal description: _____

_____ County _____.

Personal property included: _____

Earnest Money Deposit	$_____
Cash To Seller At Closing	$_____
Existing Loans & Liens	$_____
New Loan To Seller At Closing	$_____
Purchase Price	$_____

The purchase price to be paid as follows: 1. EARNEST MONEY to be deposited with licensed title company or attorney within 48 hours of acceptance by seller. The buyer will take title subject to the following loans on terms agreeable to the buyer: A. Loan to _____ Balance

$_____Interest rate: _____ %, Monthly Payment

$_____ Loan Number _____Date last payment

made_____ Loan current through _____

_____B. Loan to _____ Balance $_

_____Interest rate: _____ %, Monthly Payment

$_____ Loan Number _____Date last payment

made_____ Loan current through _____

_____Other liens: _____

_____Any overstatement in the above loan and lien amounts will be added to note to seller. Any understatement will be deducted from balance due at close.

2. THE BALANCE DUE SELLER in the amount of $ _____ shall be paid as follows: _____

_____

_____ including

interest at the rate of _____%.

3. PRORATIONS, IMPOUNDS & SECURITY DEPOSITS: Loan interest, property taxes, insurance, and rents shall be prorated as of the date of closing. All security deposits shall be transferred to buyer at closing. All impound accounts for taxes and insurance are included in the purchase price and shall be trans-

ferred to buyer at closing. Any shortage in these accounts shall be charged to seller at closing. Page 2 of 2 Purchase and Sale Agreement

4. CONDITION OF HOUSE AND APPLIANCES: Seller warrants that the house and all mechanical systems and appliances will be in good working order at closing. Buyer will have access to property for inspection and the cost of any needed repairs will be paid by seller at closing. Appliances and other personal property will be transferred by bill of sale free of encumbrances at closing.

5. CLOSING DATE AND TRANSFER OF TITLE: This transaction shall close on or before _____, 20___. Closing will be held at _____ _____ and Seller(s) agree to transfer marketable title free and clear of all encumbrances except those listed and pay any required state taxes or stamps required to record deed and mortgage. Seller agrees to furnish title insurance in the amount of the purchase price, showing no encumbrances or exceptions other than previously noted.

6. DAMAGE TO PROPERTY: Seller shall maintain property in its current condition and keep it insured against all loss until closing in the event of destruction covered by insurance, buyer may elect to close and collect the insurance proceeds.

7. DEFAULTS: If buyer defaults under this contract, any and all monies deposited by buyer(s) shall be retained by seller as full liquidated damages. If seller defaults, buyer may pursue all remedies allowed by law and seller agrees to be responsible for all costs incurred by buyer as a result of sellers default.

8. SUCCESSORS AND ASSIGNEES: The terms and conditions of this contract shall bind all successors, heirs, administrators, trustees, executors and assignees of the respective parties.

9. ACCESS ADVERTISING AND REPAIRS MADE BY BUYERS: Sellers agree that buyers may advertise property and have access during reasonable hours to show property to others. If the property is vacant and in need of repairs, buyers at their expense may make repairs and improvements, and any improvements made shall become the property of the seller should the buyer default,

10. ADDITIONAL TERMS AND CONDITIONS:

_____
_____
_____

The undersigned have read the above information, understand it and verify that it is correct.

SELLERS: _____
_____

BUYERS:_____
_____

Land Contract
(Use when buying)

This Agreement is made and entered into by and between:

_____

_____
(seller)
whose address is:

_____

_____
hereinafter called the Vendor and

_____

_____
(buyer)
whose address is:

_____

_____
hereinafter called the Vendee.
Witnessed: The Vendor, for himself, his heirs and assigns, does hereby agree to sell to the Vendee, their heirs and assigns, the following real estate commonly known as:

_____

_____
and further described; as:

together with all appurtenances, rights, privileges and easements and all buildings and fixtures in their present condition located upon said property.
1. CONTRACT PRICE. METHOD OF PAYMENT, INTEREST RATE:
In consideration whereof, the Vendee agrees to purchase the above described property for the sum of _____
_____ Dollars ($_____
), payable as follows:
The sum of $_____ as initial consideration at the time of execution of the within Land Contract, the receipt of which is hereby acknowledged, leaving a principal balance owed by Vendee of $_____ together with interest on the unpaid balance payable in consecutive monthly installments of $_____
_____ beginning on the _____ day of _____

_____20____, and on the _____ day of each and every month thereafter until said balance and interest is paid in full, or until the _____ day of _____ _____ 20_____

at which time the entire remaining balance plus accrued interest shall become due and payable. The interest on the unpaid balance due hereon shall be (___ _____ %) percent annum computed monthly, in accordance with a month amortization schedule during the life of this agreement.

Payments shall be credited first to the interest. and the remainder to the to the principal or other sums due Vendor. The total amount of this obligation, both principal and interest. unpaid after making any such application of payments as herein receipted shall be the interest bearing principal amount of this obligation for the next succeeding interest computation period. If any payment is not received within _____(_____) days of payment date, there shall be a late charge of (_____%) percent assessed. The Vendees may pay the entire purchase price on this contract without prepayment penalty. The monthly installments shall be payable as directed by the Vendor herein.

Page 2 of 3 Land Contract

2. ENCUMBRANCES:

Said real estate is presently subjeC1 to a mortgage with _____ _____ and the Vendor shall not place any additional mortgage on the premises without the prior written permission of the Vendees. To protect Vendee's interests. Vendee may elect at any time to pay any sums due hereunder directly to the mortgagee, and any amounts remaining to the Vendor. Vendor understands that this transaction may permit the mortgagee to exercise their right to accelerate the loan and to call the remaining balance due. In any such event, the Vendor agrees to hold Vendee harmless and in no way liable for any damage to Vendor as a result of such action. Vendor initials _____.

3. EVIDENCE OF TITLE:

The Vendor shall be required to provide an abstract or guarantee of title, statement of title, title insurance, or such other evidence of title to Vendee's satisfaction.

4. RECORDING OF CONTRACT:

The Vendor shall permit a copy of this contract to be recorded in the _____ _____County Recorder's Office at Vendee's discretion at any time subsequent to the execution of this Contract by the parties hereto.

5. REAL ESTATE TAXES:

Real estate taxes to the County Treasurer shall remain In the Vendor's name throughout the term of this agreement. Payment of said taxes shall be the responsibility of the Vendee upon the execution of this agreement, and [___] shall [___] shall not be escrowed and added to the payment required by Vendee herein.

6. INSURANCE AND MAINTENANCE:

The Vendor shall insure the property with a non owner-occupant (landlord) policy against fire and extended coverage to the benefit of both parties as their Interests may appear herein. Said policy shall be for an amount no less than _____, payment of which shall be the responsibility of the Vendee, and which shall be escrowed and added to the payment due herein.

Vendees shall keep the building in a good state of repair at the Vendees expense. At such time as the Vendor inspects the premises and finds that repairs are necessary, Vendor shall request that these repairs be made within sixty (60) days at the Vendees expense. The Vendees have inspected the premises constituting the subject matter of this Land Contract, and no representations have been made to the Vendee by the Vendor in regard to the condition of said premises: and it is agreed that the said premises are being sold to the Vendee as the same now exists and that the Vendor shall have no obligation to do or furnish anything toward the improvement of said premises. Vendor shall furnish a clear termite report at Vendor's expense prior to executing this contract. If the property has live infestation of wood destroying insecls, Vendor will pay costs of treatment and repair damages caused by same. If Vendor elects not to do so. Vendee may elect to waive Vendors responsibility and proceed. or Vendee may elect not to proceed with this contract. Notice of each election shall be given in writing within five (5) days of. respectively. receipt of Vendor of the notice of infestation and receipt by Vendee of Vendors notice as to intention to remedy.

7. POSSESSION

The Vendee shall be given possession of the above described premises at Contract execution and shall thereafter have and hold the same subject to default provisions hereinafter set forth.

8. Delivery of DEED:

Upon full payment of this contract, Vendor shall issue a General Warranty deed to the Vendees free of all encumbrances except as otherwise set forth. In addition, Vendees reserves the right to convert this contract into a note and mortgage which shall bear the same terms as the contract for the remaining balance, and receive a warranty Deed to Vendees or assigns from Vendor, anytime the following conditions have been met by then Vendees,

At least 20% of the purchase price has been paid to the Vendor.

Vendee is willing to pay all the costs of title transfer and document preparations.

Page 3 of 3 Land Contract

9. DEFAULT BY VENDEES

If an installment payment to be made by the Vendee under the terms of this Land Contract is not paid by the Vendee when due or within thirty (30) days thereafter, the entire unpaid balance shall become due and collectable at the election of the Vendor and the Vendor shall be entitled to all the remedies provided for by the laws of this state and/or to do any other remedies and/or seek relief now or hereafter provided for by law to such Vendor; and in the event of the breach of this contract in any other respect by the Vendee, Vendor shall be entitled to all relief now or hereinafter provided for by the laws of this state.

Failure of Vendee to maintain current the status of all real estate taxes and insurance premiums as required herein shall permit Vendor the option to pay any such premiums, taxes, interest, or penalty(ies), and to add the amount paid to the principal amount owing under this contract, or to exercise any remedies available to the Vendor as per the preceding paragraph.

Waiver by the Vendor of a default or a number of defaults in the performance hereof by the Vendee shall not be construed as a waiver of any future default no matter how similar.

10. GENERAL PROVISIONS:

There are no known pending orders issued by any governmental authority with respect to this property other than those spelled out in this Land Contract prior to closing date for the execution of the contract.

11. SPECIAL PROVISIONS:

_____

_____

_____

_____

_____

_____

12. ENTIRE AGREEMENT:

It is agreed that this instrument and any addendum mutually entered into and, by reference to this agreement, made a part hereof constitutes the entire agreement of the parties, and which shall be binding upon each of the parties, their administrators. executors, heirs and assigns. It is further agreed that neither party is relying upon any representation not contained herein.

IN WITNESS WHEREOF, the parties have set their hands this _____day of _____, 20_____,

Signed in the presence of: VENDOR: _____

_____   _____

Signed in the presence of: VENDEES: _____

_____   _____

STATE OF_____
COUNTY OF _____
On this _____ day of _____, 20____,before me, a
Notary Public in and for said county and state. personally came, _____
_____ Vendor (s) and.
_____
_____ Vendee(s) in the foregoing Land Contract. and acknowl-
edged and signing thereof to be their voluntary act and deed.
WITNESS my official signature and seal on the day last above mentioned.

_____

This instrument was prepared by: NOTARY PUBLIC

_____
_____
_____

HOME INSPECTION CHECKLIST

Address _____

Owner/Realtor_____

List Price_____ Year Built_____

Square Footage_____ Rooms LR___ DR____ BR___ Bath_____

Measurements:
Living Room_____ Dining Room_____ Kitchen_____
Bedroom 1_____ Bedroom 2 _____Bedroom 3 _____Other Room _____
__Bathroom_____Basement_____ Rec Room_____ Other_____
Other_____

Location	Notes(Type,Etc.)	Good	Fair	Poor	Comments
Exterior Landscaping					
Driveway					
Garage					
Deck					
Porches					
Roof (Type)					
Chimney					
Windows					

Location	Notes(Type,Etc.)	Good	Fair	Poor	Comments
Doors					
Interior Walls					
Flooring					
Ceilings					
Appearance					
Closets					
Kitchen					
Appliances					
Window Treatments					
Built Ins					
Heating Vents					
Mechanicals Electrical					
Furnace					
Hot Water Heater					
Air Conditioning					

Plumbing					
Other Areas Basement					
Attic					

OtherComments/Overall Impressions

Bill Of Sale for Personal Property
STATE OF_____
COUNTY OF _____
Know all men by these presents:
That the maker,_____(hereinafter
referred to as "Seller"), of this instrument for and in consideration of the sum of $_
_____Dollars in hand paid, at and before the deliv-
ery of these presents, the receipt whereof is hereby acknowledged; has bargained,
sold, transferred, conveyed and delivered, and by these presents does bargain,
sell, transfer, convey and deliver unto _____
_____ (Hereinafter referred to as "Buyer"), the following described property,
to wit:_____
_____
_____

TO HAVE AND TO HOLD the personal property above described, unto the
said Buyer, their, heirs, executors, administrators and assigns, to their only
proper use, benefit and behoove forever. The Seller fully warrants their right
and title to said property unto said Buyer, their heirs, executors, administrators
and assigns. IN WITNESS WHEREOF, Seller has hereunto set their hand and
seal this _____day of_____ 20____.
Signed, sealed and delivered in the presence of:

_____   _____

Witness   (Seal)

_____   _____

Witness

Independent Contracting Agreement

_____, referred to as
CONTRACTING PARTY,
and _____
_____, referred to as INDEPENDENT CONTRACTOR
whose mailing address is:

_____
_____
_____

and whose Social Security Number is _____
_____, agree:
INDEPENDENT CONTRACTOR shall perform the following services for
CONTRACTING PARTY on the property at _____
_____
_____
_____

Items to be supplied by the Contracting Party in sufficient quantity to complete the specified job:

_____
_____
_____
_____

This agreement shall begin on _____ and shall terminate on _____
_____ unless earlier terminated. The amount of _____/100ths
Dollars ($ _____) shall be paid if the services specified above are
completed on or before the termination date. If work is not completed on or
before the termination date without sufficient reason , _____
_____/100ths Dollars ($_____) shall be deducted from Independent
Contractor's remuneration for each day over the termination date. If work is
completed before the termination date, Independent Contractor shall receive a
bonus of _____/100ths Dollars ($_____) over
the agreed remuneration for each day before the termination date.
CONTRACTING PARTY may terminate this contract on twenty four (24)
hours notice to INDEPENDENT CONTRACTOR for unsatisfactory performance.
THIS IS AN AGREEMENT FOR INDEPENDENT CONTRACTING
SERVICES. THE CONTRACTING PARTY PROVIDES NO BENEFITS SUCH
AS UNEMPLOYMENT INSURANCE, HEALTH INSURANCE, OR WORKER'S
COMPENSATION INSURANCE TO INDEPENDENT CONTRACTOR.

CONTRACTING PARTY IS ONLY INTERESTED IN THE RESULTS OBTAINED BY THE INDEPENDENT CONTRACTOR. INDEPENDENT CONTRACTOR SHALL BE RESPONSIBLE FOR PROVIDING ALL LABOR, TOOLS, AND UNSPECIFIED MATERIALS REQUIRED FOR PERFORMANCE OF THE TASKS AGREED TO.

INDEPENDENT CONTRACTOR IS RESPONSIBLE FOR PROVIDING WORKER'S COMPENSATION INSURANCE FOR THEMSELVES AND THEIR EMPLOYEES. THE INDEPENDENT CONTRACTOR IS ALSO RESPONSIBLE FOR THE PAYMENT OF ALL FEDERAL, STATE AND LOCAL INCOME TAXES.

Dated: _____

_____   _____

Contracting Party By An Authorized Officer

Real Estate Terms

adjustable rate mortgage (ARM)
Type of home loan where the interest rate varies over time based on changes in the treasury bill rate. The initial period of the loan may be set at an interest rate but rates will begin to increase or decrease based on the federal rate. These loans are also considered variable rate mortgages.

amortization schedule
A schedule or timetable for payments of a mortgage loan. The amortization schedule shows the amount of each payment and what part of the payment is principle and what part is interest

amortization term
The amount of time required to amortize the mortgage loan. The amortization term is expressed as a number of months. For example, for a 30-year fixed-rate mortgage, the amortization term is 360 months.

annual percentage rate (APR)
The cost of a mortgage stated as a yearly rate; includes such items as interest, mortgage insurance and loan origination fee (points).

annuity
An amount paid yearly or at other regular intervals, often on a guaranteed dollar basis.

appraisal
A written estimate of the fair market value of a property prepared by a qualified appraiser. Banks use appraisals to confirm a property value in underwriting.

appreciation
Increases in the value of a property due to changes in market conditions, rising demand, renovation, and expansion. The opposite of depreciation.

assessed value
The value placed on property by a public tax assessor for the purposes of taxation.

assessment
The process of placing a value on property for the strict purpose of taxation. May also refer to a levy against property for a special purpose, such as a sewer assessment.

assumable mortgage
A type of mortgage that can be taken over by a new buyer when the original home is sold. Very beneficial to investors because this may be a way to lock in a low rate or get additional financing.

basis
Used for tax purposes as a beginning point that depreciation or capital gains begins.

broker's commission
The fee charged by the real estate agent to list, market, and sell a property.

capitalization rate (cap rate)
This is the rate of return of an income producing property. The formula to determine this rate is taking the net operating income minus the operating expenses.

capital improvement
Any structure or component erected as a permanent improvement to real property that adds to its value and useful life.

cash-out refinance
A way to refinance a property and pull out money from the house. This occurs when the money received from the new loan is greater than the money needed to pay off existing first mortgage, closing costs, and other fees. Some lenders may only allow you to borrow 75% or 80% of the home's value on a cash out refinance.

clear title
Also known as clean title. Means that the title that is free of liens or other issues that would question ownership of property.

closing
The meeting where the paperwork is signed to transfer ownership of a property.

closing costs
Fees associated with closing the sale of a property. These fees can be any of the following: title fees, pre-paid interest, loan closing fees, realtor fees, etc.
help the appraiser determine the approximate fair market value of the subject property.

CLUE Report
A report that is prepared by the private Comprehensive Loss Underwriting Exchange and gives a history of home ownership insurance claims on a property.

contingency
A condition that must be met before a contract is legally binding. For example, home purchasers often include a contingency that specifies that the contract is

not binding until the purchaser obtains a satisfactory termite inspection report from an inspector.

credit report

A detailed report of a person's credit history prepared by one of the major credit bureaus and used by a lender to determine loan eligibility. Credit reports may be obtained from Equifax, Experian, or Transunion. Some agencies also do 3 in 1 credit reports.

credit score

This is the score give by the credit reporting agency to determine your credit worthiness. The higher the score the better. Scores range from 300-800. This scores is also referred to as your FICO score.

curb appeal

How well the house looks from the outside. Curb appeal is an impression that the house gives.

deed

The legal document conveying title to a property. It is typically registered by the city clerk of courts.

deed in lieu of foreclosure

A deed given by the owner to the bank to avoid foreclosure. This satisfies the owner's debt to the lender.

of a loan. See earnest money deposit.

depreciation

Has two meanings: 1. A decline in the value of property; the opposite of appreciation. 2. Can be a tax write off to the IRS when a property is used as an investment. As the property is used it declines in value. Owners can write off portions of depreciation over time to save in taxes.

earnest money deposit

A deposit made by a buyer to show that he or she is serious about buying the house.

easement

A right of way giving persons other than the owner access to or over a property.

encumbrance

Anything that affects or limits the fee simple title to a property, such as mortgages, leases, easements or restrictions.

equity

The value that is owned in a property. Equity is the difference between the fair market value of the property and the amount still owed on its mortgage.

escrow

When parties agree to allow a third party to hold an item of value, money, or documents. This third party will deliver the items after all conditions are met.

exclusive right to sell

The exclusive listing agreement between the owner and real estate agent that ensures a payment of a commission to the real estate agent during a specified period of time.

fair market value

The value of a property that is the highest price that a buyer would be willing to pay for a property and the lowest that the seller would accept.

Fannie Mae

An agency set up to ensure mortgages flow steadily into the market. Fannie Mae is the biggest investor in mortgage loans. Fannie Mae along with HUD have created buying guidelines to ensure equal housing standards.

Federal Housing Administration (FHA)

FHA is an agency of the U.S. Department of Housing and Urban Development (HUD). Its main activity is the insuring of residential mortgage loans made by private lenders.

foreclosure

A process that an owner in default of a mortgage undergoes so the bank can either get their defaulted payments plus penalties or takeover the property. This may involve a public sale or a forced takeover.

FSBO

means For Sale By Owner

general contractor

A contractor that oversees the completion of a project. May not be a specialist and may hire other subcontractors to help complete work.

home equity line of credit

A type of mortgage loan, usually a second, that allows gives the owner a line of credit that is secured by the home.

home inspection

A detailed inspection done by a home inspector that evaluates the structural and mechanical condition of a property. This is a visual inspection usually obtained by the buyer to assess the condition of a property.

home warranty

A limited warranty or type of insurance will cover repairs to a house over a specified period of time.

HUD-1 settlement statement
The final settlement statement prepared for the closing that gives the costs of purchase, closing costs, and proceeds to the seller. This is a legal document that can be used to help prepare your taxes.
rate used to calculate the monthly payments, although it is not used for an adjustable-rate

interest rates
The rates charged when you borrow money.

joint tenancy
A type of co-ownership that gives each tenant equal interest and equal rights in the property, including the right of survivorship.

judgment
A decision that could show up on title where the court has made a decision on the debt of another. Judgments require a repayment of a lien before a clear title will be given.

judicial foreclosure
A foreclosure proceeding used by some states when the foreclosure is treated like a civil lawsuit and handled through the courts in a legal process.

lease
The written legal agreement between the property owner and a tenant that stipulates the conditions that the tenant can occupy a property, the amount of rent, and penalties for non compliance.

lien
A legal claim on a property that must be paid off at the time the property is sold.

loan commitment
A final letter or commitment from the lender that they will finance a loan. Usually contains rates on terms that the loan is given.

loan to value ratio
The amount loaned against a property versus its value.

mortgage
A loan that is used to purchase real estate. It is a legal document that gives the lender the authority to use the property as security for repayment of the loan.

mortgage banker
A company that originates mortgages and then resale's them in the secondary mortgage market.

mortgage broker
A person or company that works with buyers to help them secure a mortgage loan from a bank. This broker may work with numerous banks and does not

service the loan after the loan closes. Mortgage brokers are paid a fee for their service.

multifamily properties

An apartment building or property that has multiple dwelling units.

net operating income

The income received from a rental property after operating expenses are subtracted but before subtracting income taxes and mortgage expenses.

owner occupied

The term used when the property is lived in by the owners.

decrease during any one adjustment period.

PITI

The acronym for principal, interest, taxes and insurance. This is the total payment that would be paid.

point

A fee charged by a lender for originating a loan. A point is 1 percent of the amount of the mortgage.

pre-foreclosure sale

A process that the lender allows the borrower to avoid foreclosure by selling the property for less than the amount that is owed to the lender.

prepayment penalty

A penalty fee charged to a borrower when he pays off a loan early or before it's due.

principal

The actual amount that is included in the mortgage. This is the only part of the monthly payment that reduces the remaining balance of a mortgage.

private mortgage insurance (PMI)

Insurance required by a bank when the buyer does not put down 20% on a property or have 20% equity in a property.

property manager

A person or company that may assist the owner with managing the maintenance and rent collection of a property. Can serve as a liaison to the property owner.

public auction

A meeting in an announced public location to sell property to repay a mortgage that is in default.

quitclaim deed

A deed that may be granted without a guarantee of clear title.

real estate agent

A person who is licensed to negotiate and transact the sale of real estate on behalf a property owner. Can be a buyer's agent, seller's agent, or dual agent. A

REALTOR is active with the National Association of REALTORs and adheres to a strict code of ethics.

recording
The noting in the registrar's office of the details of a properly executed legal document, such as a deed, a mortgage note, a satisfaction of mortgage or an extension of mortgage, thereby making it a part of the public record.

real estate owned (REO)
Real estate that has been foreclosed on and is now retained by the bank.

seller carry back
A type of mortgage loan where the seller holds a second mortgage on the property. This is also referred to as a seller second.

sweat equity
Equity that is gained in a property by physical upgrades to the property.

title company
A company that specializes in examining and insuring titles to real estate.

title insurance
The warranty or insurance instrument that will protect the owner's rights to the property.

title search
A search performed by the title company to insure the property has clear title. to be a transfer of ownership: the purchase of a property "subject to" the mortgage, the

transfer tax
The State or local tax that is due when title passes from one owner to another.

978-0-595-40436-0
0-595-40436-7

www.ingramcontent.com/pod-product-compliance
Lightning Source LLC
Chambersburg PA
CBHW030948180526
45163CB00002B/711